Thomas Beddoes

Observations on the nature of demonstrative evidence with an explanation of certain difficulties occurring in the elements of geometry and reflections on language

Thomas Beddoes

Observations on the nature of demonstrative evidence with an explanation of certain difficulties occurring in the elements of geometry and reflections on language

ISBN/EAN: 9783742824486

Manufactured in Europe, USA, Canada, Australia, Japa

Cover: Foto ©Thomas Meinert / pixelio.de

Manufactured and distributed by brebook publishing software
(www.brebook.com)

Thomas Beddoes

Observations on the nature of demonstrative evidence with an explanation of certain difficulties occurring in the elements of geometry and reflections on language

OBSERVATIONS

ON THE NATURE OF

DEMONSTRATIVE EVIDENCE;

WITH AN

EXPLANATION OF CERTAIN DIFFICULTIES

OCCURRING IN THE

ELEMENTS OF GEOMETRY:

AND

REFLECTIONS ON LANGUAGE.

By THOMAS BEDDOES.

En general, dans les mathematiques on ne s'arrête pas a resoudre les difficultés metaphysiques, qui se presentent. . . . . . : . . M. TURGOT eût voulu qu'on dissipât jusqu'aux plus petites obscurités. *Vie de Turgot.*

LONDON:

PRINTED FOR J. JOHNSON, Nº 72, IN ST. PAUL'S CHURCH-YARD. 1793.

TO

DAVIES GIDDY, Esq.

DEAR GIDDY,

FOR the principal opinion, ſtated and exemplified in the following pages, it ſeems to me that I have the full evidence of intuition; and this evidence, you know, muſt always carry conviction to the mind of the individual. All he can deſire further is to learn, whether objects appear to the ſenſes of others as they appear to his ſenſes.

What additional confirmation it is poſſible in ſuch circumſtances to receive, was afforded me by your aſſent, when I formerly mentioned to you my ideas concerning demonſtrative evidence. Your uncommon proficiency in mathematical ſcience, and your no leſs uncommon diſcernment, I was well aſſured, perfectly qualified you to decide on ſuch a queſtion.

To thoſe who catch an idea the inſtant it is preſented, and who have facts in abundance at command, by which they can determine the validity of a principle, I ſhall frequently appear tedious. That ungrateful feeling, I will own to you, oftener than once while I was writing, came acroſs my mind. But you are at no loſs to conceive the manner in which I would defend my prolixity. What I have written, if it ſhould obtain regard, will be viewed by moſt readers with an eye of ſuſpicion; and

by

by many, if they follow their firſt movement, it will be rejected as paradoxical. Will not ſuch conſiderations as theſe juſtify a variety of illuſtrations, and even repetitions?—They have alſo induced me to run the riſque of appearing ridiculouſly minute, in tracing the origin of terms.

Fortunately for the diffuſion of juſt ſentiments, Mr. Harris has loſt that authority which even among the learned he maintained too long. Our young men, however, I believe, ſtill frequently reſort to HERMES for that inſtruction, which he has not to ſupply. For obſerve, I beſeech you, what they will learn from this once redoubted doctor of *univerſals*, concerning mathematical reaſoning.—" It is ſome-" what remarkable," ſays he, ſarcaſtically glancing at the attention paid to the phyſical ſciences, " amid the prevalence of " ſuch notions, that there ſhould ſtill re-

" main

"main two ſciences in faſhion, and theſe "having their certainty of all the leaſt "controverted, *which are not in the mi-* "*nuteſt article depending upon experiment.* "By theſe I mean ARITHMETIC and GEO- "METRY." In a curious note, but which is too long to be inſerted entire, he has the inſolence to ſubjoin, "I would not be "underſtood, in what I have here ſaid, "or may have ſaid elſewhere, to under- "value EXPERIMENT; whoſe importance "and utility I freely acknowledge, in the "many curious noſtrums and choice re- "ceipts, with which it has enriched the "neceſſary arts of life. Nay, I go far- "ther—I hold *all juſtifiable practice in every* "*kind of ſubject* to be founded in EXPE- "RIENCE, which is no more than the re- "ſult of *many repeated* EXPERIMENTS. . . . . "In the mean time, while EXPERIMENT "is thus neceſſary to all PRACTICAL WIS-

"DOM,

"DOM, with respect to all PURE and SPE-
"CULATIVE SCIENCE, it has not the least
"to do. For who ever heard of *Logic*, or
"*Geometry*, or *Arithmetic* being proved *ex-
"perimentally* * ?" That the affirmations of Mr. Harris may lose nothing of their effect, they are here introduced in all their native pomp of CAPITALS and archness of *italics*.

The more I consider the subject, the more I am inclined, in spite of Mr. Harris, to believe not only in the possibility, but the utility of rendering the elements of geometry palpable. If they be taught at an early age — a plan in which I think I see many advantages—models would make the study infinitely more engaging: From the mere slate and pencil most beginners experience a repulsive sensation. But if a child had something to handle and to place in

* Hermes, p. 351-3.

various

various poſtures, he might learn many properties of geometrical figures without any conſtraint upon his inclinations. He would have no difficulty in transferring the properties of palpable to merely viſible figures, nor in generalizing the inferences. *You* will not object, that one cannot proceed far by this road: you will perceive, that much more would be gained in reality than appearance. We ſhould have laid a good foundation for the invaluable habit of accurate obſervation in general; and towards future progreſs in mathematics, we ſhould have warded off the firſt diſagreeable impreſſion of the aſpect of the ſcience, which is ſo very apt to ſtrike a damp to the heart of the beginner.

I need not explain to you the advantage of trying to engage Fancy on our ſide, by all the allurements we can offer to her. It is ſhe that ſmooths every path and ſtrews

it

it with flowers. We all, men and boys, follow with alacrity wherever ſhe leads; neither the mind, nor the body, grudge any labour; and it is the enthuſiaſm ſhe inſpires, that has worked ſo many miracles in art and ſcience. By ſome ſtrange fatality however, ſhe is neglected, if not affronted in almoſt all the ſtages of education; and the firſt ſtep in almoſt every ſpecies of inſtruction is, to preſent knowledge to the ſtudent's imagination, in conjunction with ſome melancholy and hateful accompaniment; which ſort of management, I conceive to have much the ſame kindly influence upon this faculty, as an unſeaſonable froſt upon the tender petals of an expanding bloſſom.

The mode of initiation in geometry which I propoſe, could not, unleſs I very much deceive myſelf, fail to render the impreſſions of ſenſe more agreeable by rendering them more diſtinct. The *rigorouſly ſcien-*

tific method, as it is ſuppoſed to be, ſeems, on the contrary, to aim only at rendering them as obſcure as poſſible : an intention, I confeſs, perfectly in uniſon with the other parts of the eſtabliſhed proceſs of SCHOOL and COLLEGE ſtupefaction.

Whether you will allow that this important point is likely to be in this manner attained, I am not ſure. But you will agree with me in thinking, that it is high time to diſcard Euclid's Elements. The ſcience cannot be exhibited in a more diſguſting form ; as we may be convinced by daily inſtances. Nor are theſe Elements any way neceſſary to lay a good foundation in mathematics, for there are few, I will venture to gueſs, of the eminent mathematicians of Europe, that have been initiated by the ſtudy of Euclid.

That by laying Euclid aſide, we ſhould be deprived of what Bacon calls the intervenient advantages of mathematics, is to me a vain a vain apprehenſion. Thoſe who have dragged their underſtanding laboriouſly along the tireſome circuit of ancient demonſtration, may be unwilling to grant, that they have taken all theſe pains to no purpoſe. Yet they can hardly flatter themſelves in ſecret, that they have acquired habits of attention or abſtraction ſuperior to thoſe, who having preſſed forward by the neareſt road, enjoy both the direct and indirect profits of their labour.

For want of time or opportunity or reſolution, I am not able to take ſo comprehenſive a view of the ſubject as I could wiſh. I cannot indeed ſuppoſe it poſſible, that either branch of mathematics ſhould ever ceaſe to be

Qualis ab incepto proceſſerit;

but I am apprehenſive, that I have not preſented my obſervations in ſo advantageous a form as I might have done, if I had poſſeſſed more knowledge. I hope, however,

to

to be intelligible to thofe who may choofe to examine them. In the main principle I cannot fuppofe myfelf miftaken; where I have committed errors in the application, I fhall receive correction with the chearfulnefs becoming a perfon, equally ready to hear and tell the truth.

I am,

With fincere regard,

DEAR GIDDY,

Your's,

Oxford.
Sept. 6, 1792.

THOMAS BEDDOES.

OBSER-

OBSERVATIONS

ON THE NATURE OF

DEMONSTRATIVE

OR

MATHEMATICAL EVIDENCE.

IN proportion as the writings of Mr. Locke rose in the public esteem, Ontology and the old Logic appear to have declined: the memorable improvements in physical knowledge, which took place about his time, and those which have since been made, by offering far different objects to curiosity, co-operated with Mr. Locke's endeavours to bring that unprofitable jargon into disrepute. Such has been the happy effect of these conspiring causes, that the world has been delivered from its long subjection to empty sounds; the talent of wrangling is no longer considered as the grand object of education; and the means of acquiring this talent have been, by general consent, cast aside into those lumber-rooms of learning, THE SCHOOLS.

Mr. Locke's success has, I imagine, already contributed, and will hereafter, in a greater degree still, contribute to render his ESSAY less popular; for one may, without impropriety, call a book popular that has gone through twenty editions. The scholastic learning, which he occasionally introduces on purpose to expose it, is now little familiar to the majority of his readers; and to those readers who are not accustomed to its terms, many passages will be obscure and uninterefting. This great work contains, however, obfcurities, depending on a lefs honourable caufe: the author fometimes attempts to explain what he does not underftand, and fometimes, with wonderful unfteadinefs, half abandons his own principles. It has lately been fhewn, that his capital miftake was concerning language. Hence as he did not throw light enough upon this important fubject to moleft the grammarians in their operations, they ftill worked on in the true fpirit of their brethren, the fchoolmen; and by their diftinctions elucidated the nature of words, about as much as the fchoolmen had advanced the knowledge of things by their fyllogifms.

At laft the Επεα Πτεροεντα of Mr. Horne Tooke diffipated the clouds left by the Effay on the Human Underftanding; and the foundations of knowledge were laid fairly open to thofe, who fhould have the curioſity to inſpect them. It was by deciſively ſhewing, that we have no general or complex ideas, and that every word in language, (interjections excepted, which are hardly entitled to the appellation of words,) ſignifies ſome object or perception of ſenſe, that Mr. Tooke compleated what Mr. Locke had begun. Mr. Locke indeed did every thing but make the diſcovery himſelf. According to his negative definition of the general idea of a triangle, "it muſt be "neither oblique, nor rectangle, neither "equilateral, equicrural, nor ſcalenon, but "all and none of theſe at once." It was eaſy, one might at firſt ſight ſuppoſe, to infer that the human mind is incapable of conceiving ſuch an idea; and hence that general terms are not ſigns of general ideas, but a contrivance to avoid a multitude of uſeleſs names, and that complex terms denote no fixed ideas like thoſe ariſing from external

objects

objects or impressions of sense, but that each shortly denotes a number of simple perceptions or sensations, for which reason their import is apt to vary extremely, as they are used by different persons.

In whatever study you are engaged, to leave difficulties behind, is distressing; and when these difficulties occur at your very entrance upon a science, professing to be so clear and certain as geometry, your feelings become still more uncomfortable: and you are dissatisfied with your own powers of comprehension. I, therefore, think it due to the author of ΕΠΕΑ ΠΤΕΡΟΕΝΤΑ to acknowledge my obligations to him for relieving me from this sort of distress. For although I had often enough made the attempt, I could never solve certain difficulties in Euclid, till my reflections were revived and assisted by Mr. Tooke's discoveries.—I have indeed lately learned, that a doctrine concerning language, partly the same as that of Mr. Tooke, had been for some time taught in the celebrated school of Greek literature at Leyden. Mr. Hemſterhuis, and his diſciples, had ſucceſsfully traced many words of that language to their primary *ſenſible* ſignification; and they expreſs themſelves with precision on the manner * of

* For inſtance, Lennep (Etymol. p. 7.) ſays: Notiones verborum *propriæ* omnes ſunt *corporeæ*, ſive ad *res* pertinentes, quæ ſenſus noſtros feriunt.—Quæ, præter verba et nomina, numerantur *partes orationis*, ea, vel ad verba, vel ad nomina, proprie referenda ſunt; niſi ſint quædam *interjectiones*. (id. ibid. p. 8.)—From Scaliger, Mr. Scheid adopts this principle: unius vocis *una* tantum eſt ſignificatio propria et princeps. (Animad, ad Analog. p. 351.)——Again, Valde veriſimile fit, vocabula ea in linguis antiquiſſima eſſe, quibus res deſignantur, ad vitam degendam neceſſariæ——

Porro non alienum erit, hic obſervaſſe non tantum ejuſmodi vocabula antiquiſſima exiſtimari debere, ſed etiam *ipſas* ſignificationes, verbis ſubjectas, tanto antiquioris uſus eſſe, tantoque magis proprias eſſe habendas, quanto ſunt propriores iis rebus, quas, corporis ſenſibus, percipimus. Ab iis enim ſemper, ſervatâ quâdam ſimilitudine, ad reliquas quaſcumque verborum ſignificationes, progrediendum eſt: ut adeo appareat pauciſſimas revera eſſe *proprias* verborum ſignificationes;

of signification of words. The grammatical researches however of the eminent Greek

ficationes; nec alias esse nisi *corporeas* sive eas, quibus res sensibus exterius expositæ, designantur. E contrario autem, translatarum significationum copiam immensam, quæ ex *propriâ* notione, tanquam ex trunco arboris rami, quaquaversum pateant. *Lennep. Anal.* p. 41.

As Mr. Tooke has not yet satisfied the curiosity of the public by illustrating the manner of signification of the pronouns, and those who have followed him as far as he has hitherto gone, must be extremely desirous to understand the construction of this part of language, I will subjoin an instance which perhaps may give the reader an idea how the pronouns arise, and what is their primary sensible signification.

Tot in Coptic signifies *hand*. See Woide Lexicon Ægypt. who goes on to say, *usurpatur instar nominis possessivi*, and then quotes several Coptic phrases, in which he translates Tot by the possessive pronoun. Then by a prefix of the letter N, of which the primary sense is not known, it signifies *to have*, *to possess*: as,

 " Ntot,

Greek ſcholars, who have flouriſhed in Holland, are, if we except thoſe of Schultens, but

"Ντοτ, habere, ἔχειν.—as Matt. xxi. 26. Ιωαννης γαρ ΝΤΟΤου ὡς ουπροφητης, habent enim Johannem ſicuti prophetam."

In his Grammat. Egypt. p. 38, he ſays "τοτ, manus, ντοτ, manus mea, i. e. ego, Pſalm cxxx. 8. ετοτ, mihi, Syrac. xxiv. 8. Δατοτεp, inter nos." With other ſuffixes it is uſed to expreſs the other perſons. Two or three other words, of which I do not find the primary ſenſe, are uſed alſo for the firſt pronoun poſſeſſive. Theſe other Coptic words might ſignify *hand* among ſome of the tribes, of which the Egyptian nation, like every other, was probably formed: or other actions, beſides taking a thing into the hand, might denote poſſeſſion, and hence a derivation of pronouns from words of other ſignification.

How the familiar action of ſeizing any thing for food or other uſe might ſuggeſt an emblematic action, as in the ceremony of marriage; how this act might alſo ſuggeſt an hieroglyphic for poſſeſſion; and how eaſily the word *hand* might ſupply ſpoken and written language but beginning to be known abroad; and they appear to have adulterated the truth by the admixture of ſeveral highly improbable hypotheſes *.

The

language with poſſeſſive pronouns, every perſon will at once perceive. Suppoſing the Coptic likely to ſupply primary ſignifications, I ſearched for this purpoſe what Dr. Woide has publiſhed of this language: he muſt be reſponſible himſelf for the accuracy of his interpretation.—ΟΥΟΗ ſignifies as well *and*, as *addi*, *augeri*. The coincidence of the primary ſenſe of this conjunction in Engliſh and Egyptian is ſatisfactory, but by no means ſurpriſing.

* Readers, attached to theſe ſpeculations, will find abundant entertainment in *Valkenarii Obſervationes*, &c. *Lennepii Prælectiones Acad.* and particularly in his *Etymologicum*, all publiſhed by Prof. Scheid, in 1790. A German critic, in whoſe ſtrictures one can hardly fail to recognize Mr. Heyne, has pointed out two or three of theſe extraordinary hypotheſes. See Gotting. Anzeig. 1791, p. 578, &c. He obſerves that it is juſt as probable that the great bulk of the Greek language was

derived

The pretensions of the abstract sciences have, it must be confessed, something wonderfully alluring. In thinking they seem to promise, to speculative minds, a sort of

derived from *monads* as from the *duads*, which these writers and Lord Monboddo assign as the primitives, viz. αω, εω, ιω, οω, and ύω; for, continues he, from δω we may have δαω, διω, δυω; and we have still in the language ζω, λω, ιω, and other such monosyllables. This regularity, too, he observes in the formation of the language must, according to the Dutch doctrine, necessarily have existed among the Savages of Greece, a supposition, contrary to every argument, supplied either by physiology or psychology. He might have added, that the doctrine not only implies this supposition, but that the authors express it: as Valckenaer, p. 34, *primigeniæ significationes* a SAPIENTIBUS ISTIS LINGUÆ CONDITORIBUS *verbis impressæ——labentibus annis, deleri cœperunt*, &c. so that Horace, if he had but known this, when he said, "that many bold warriors lived before Agamemnon," might have added, "and wise philosophers too, who held councils to provide of independance upon external things, ſimilar to what ſome moraliſts have ſought to acquire in acting. And who is there, ſo immerſed in matter as to feel no deſire of ſpiritualizing the groſs body of his experi-

vide ways and means for the regular conſtruction of language!" A fact, doubtleſs, far more extraordinary.

It is alſo, as Mr. H. further remarks, very little probable that nouns were at firſt derived from verbs, as, for inſtance, that φλεγω ſhould have preceded φλοξ, or πτερυσσω, πτερυξ; abſent objects muſt have a name (hence nouns would be firſt formed), whereas actions could be imitated by geſture. It is not however to be denied, that other nouns were afterwards formed from verbs. Mr. H. ſeems to be miſtaken, in ſuppoſing that monoſyllables and diſſyllables precede polyſyllables; for, 1. In the ſpecimens of barbarous languages, of which we have lately received ſo many, you will hardly find a monoſyllable and few ſhort words; and, 2. Many imitative words muſt be long, becauſe the ſounds themſelves are long; they would be gradually ſhortened by uſe.

mental

mental knowledge, by infusing into it a diviner spark from Ontology? Whatever be his pursuit, the ambition of that scholar must be very low in its aims, who should not aspire to catch one glimpse of the pure essences of things, as they are presented by the mirror of metaphysics. But if it should appear, that the ontologists have mistaken the humble *posteriori* for the high *priori* road; that they are just as dependant upon sense and matter, as the merest experimenter; that they have laboured to no better purpose than to cloak the simplest indications of sense in a fantastic garb; and that even the claim of their subtleties to serve as a whetstone of a finer grain to the mind is groundless, since the habit of discrimination, as well as that of fixed attention, is to be perfectly acquired by studies, that are also capable of useful application; if for such reasons as these we may calmly be-

hold

hold Ontology ſinking into that grave, in which Alchemy lies buried, ſtill there will remain an abſtract ſcience, which has ſtood the competition of the phyſical ſciences, and indeed has grown with their growth. In *mathematical* reaſoning, the mind graſps the concluſions with full aſſurance of their reality; we are ſatisfied, that our advances in this ſcience are actual acquiſitions, and we find them as we go on continually capable of application.

It may therefore be intereſting to enquire into thoſe circumſtances which conſtitute the irreſiſtable force of mathematical evidence. We ſhall at the ſame time, if we are ſucceſsful in this enquiry, diſcover upon what depends the difference in the cogency of proof between demonſtrative evidence, and ſuch evidence as leſs powerfully commands our aſſent. Without this, I do not ſee how we can ever

take

take a clear ſurvey of evidence in general, or enjoy the ſatisfaction of accounting to ourſelves fully for our own conviction or belief.

It ſeems to me, in the preſent ſtate of our knowledge, ſo eaſy to point out the nature of this and the other ſorts of evidence, that I wonder how it can be miſtaken. Yet frequently as the topic is expatiated upon, I know no book in which the true principles have been fully explained and applied; and in general, I have reaſon to believe that very erroneous ideas prevail upon a ſubject, of unqueſtionable importance to the theory of the human underſtanding. I might recite the opinions of a conſiderable number of writers, and offer arguments againſt them. But if I ſucceed in eſtabliſhing my own, I ſhall at the ſame time ſufficiently refute what I imagine to be the miſtakes of others; and the reader will

at

at once perceive how far each is wide of the truth, for all are not equally wide.

On examining a train of mathematical reaſoning, we ſhall find, that at every ſtep we proceed upon the evidence of the ſenſes; or, to expreſs myſelf in different terms, I hope to be able to ſhew *that the mathematical ſciences are ſciences of experiment and obſervation, founded ſolely upon the induction of particular facts, as much ſo as mechanics, aſtronomy, optics or chemiſtry.* In the kind of evidence there is no difference; for it originates from perception in all theſe caſes alike, but mathematical experiments are more ſimple and more perfectly within the graſp of our ſenſes, and our perceptions of mathematical objects are clearer. So great indeed is the ſimplicity of mathematical experiments, that at whatever moment we are called upon to reaſon from them, we have the reſult of many of them diſtinctly

in

in our memory; the obſervations caſually made in the courſe of life, leave a ſufficient conviction of their truth upon the mind; and we are beforehand ſo fully ſatisfied as ſeldom to take the trouble of repeating them. The apparatus is ſimple: no motion or change admoniſhes us, that we are engaged in an experimental enquiry; and this is, I ſuppoſe, the reaſon why we are ſo little aware of the nature of the intellectual proceſs we are going through. Sometimes, however, notwithſtanding we are ſo well prepared, we do repeat ſome of theſe experiments; and there have probably been few teachers of geometry, who have not, at the beginning of their lectures, deſired their pupils to repeat certain fundamental experiments, till they ſhould have ſatisfied themſelves as to the reſult.

No ſooner do we look into an elementary treatiſe for the proofs of this opinion, than

than we meet with them at every ſtep in every demonſtration; and I ſhall, I hope, be allowed to have eſtabliſhed it firmly, if I ſhew that Euclid ſets out from experiments, and proceeds onwards by their aid, appealing conſtantly to what we have already learned from the exerciſe of our ſenſes, or may immediately learn. The ſame thing muſt needs be equally true of every other elementary author. After having exemplified the nature of demonſtrative reaſoning, I ſhall leave the reader to extend this mode of conſidering it to other caſes, in a full perſuaſion that he will find the ſame proceſs repeated, in every demonſtration upon which he may chooſe to make the trial. In order therefore to avoid needleſs repetition, I ſhall paſs on, and, *ſecondly*, apply the principle to the ſolution of certain difficulties in the elements of geometry, about which a great deal has

C been

been written. It will appear, that neither the doctrine of parallel lines, nor the fifth definition of the fifth book, on which Euclid founds his reaſoning concerning proportion, have any thing obſcure or doubtful, when properly conſidered. *Laſtly*, to take off that gloſs of novelty, which ſo much ſcandalizes mankind, when truth appears before their eyes for the firſt time, I ſhall ſhew that Mr. Locke has diſtinctly announced the ſame opinion. The reader may therefore, if he chooſes, conſider what follows as a commentary, upon a paſſage of Mr. Locke, which was totally loſt upon me, and, as it appears, upon others. A good commentary would prevent or relieve much perplexity.

I am firſt to review the outſet of Euclid's reaſoning, in order to ſhew that he begins from experiments, and proceeds by experiments. Theſe experiments may, indeed,

indeed, be called *mental* experiments, ſince the appeal is made to recollection, and they are commonly repeated in thought. But they are not at all more independant of experience than my acquired knowledge of the reſult of an experiment with a balance of which one arm ſhould be ten inches, and the other one inch long, and each arm ſhould be loaded in an inverſe proportion to its length: or, to take another example, ſuppoſe a train of reaſoning were to ſet out on the ſuppoſition of iron yielding hydrogene air, while it is diſſolving in vitriolic acid of a certain ſtrength, I ſhould moſt aſſuredly not think it neceſſary to repeat the experiment. Now juſt as familiar as ſuch reſult is to a perſon at all converſant in chemiſtry, juſt ſo familiar to every perſon, at leaſt every one arrived at the years of diſcretion, and having the uſe of his hands and eyes, are many of the experiments of geometry.

The fourth propoſition of the firſt book is the firſt theorem occurring in the elements of Euclid; this propoſition, and the axiom as it is called, upon which the demonſtration is founded, viz. the 10th in Simſon's edition, may be regarded as the corner-ſtone of geometrical reaſoning. The propoſition is this:

If two triangles have two ſides of the one equal to two ſides of the other each to each; and have likewiſe the angles contained by thoſe ſides equal to one another, they ſhall have their baſes, or third ſides, *equal*; *and the two triangles ſhall be equal*; *and their other angles ſhall be equal, each to each, viz. thoſe to which the equal ſides are oppoſite.*

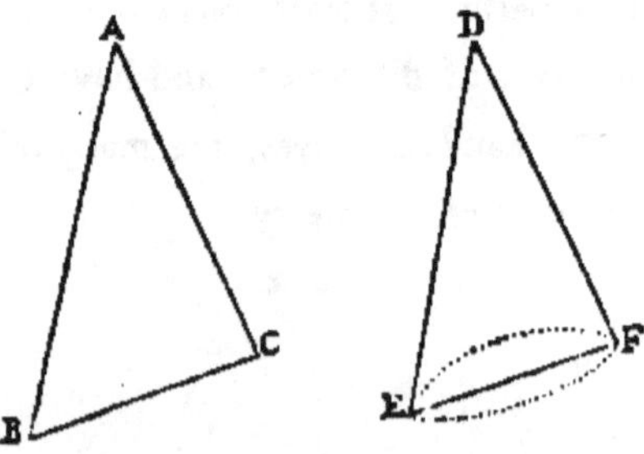

It

It will be granted, that the ideas of a triangle, of equal or unequal expanſions between lines meeting at a point, and of the equal or unequal length of different ſtraight lines, are all acquired by the exerciſe of the ſenſes. It is, indeed, evident, that we cannot in any other way acquire them.——

Now the ſide AB being made equal to DE, and AC to DF, and the angles BAC and EDF being equal, let us obſerve the experimental proceſs of the demonſtration.

If you have a model of each triangle cut out in paſteboard, or any other material, you are to place the point A upon D, which is to commence an experiment; if the triangles be only traced upon a ſurface, you are to imagine A placed upon D, which is to imagine the commencement of an experiment. Then you are to lay AB along DE; now B will fall upon E. "Why?"

becauſe from experiments or obſervations already made, you know that if you have two ſtraight ſtrips of wood, for inſtance, and put the end of one exactly over the end of the other, and turn the upper ſtrip in the direction of the lower, the other end will neither over-reach nor fall ſhort of the other end of the lower, but lie exactly over it: and this is what we mean by equality of length, a term ſolely derived from ſuch experiments of menſuration, made in early life.

To ſhew by experiment, likewiſe, which alone can ſhew it, what an angle is, and moreover that, if the line AC ſtretches as much from AB as DE does from DF, AC muſt lie along DF, whenever AB lies along DE, a carpenter's ruler may be opened and ſhut to various angles, and one carpenter's ruler may be placed over another.

This

This experiment having been performed till the reſult is allowed and underſtood, it will be ſeen that the point C muſt fall upon F, from the equality of the lines AC and DF.

Then BC muſt fall upon EF; "and why?"—make the experiment; you cannot place two ſtraight ſticks, or trace two ſtraight lines, ſo ~~they~~ as to encompaſs a ſpace, try as long as you pleaſe and ſatisfy yourſelf: if you were to try to incloſe a piece of land by two ſtraight hedges, you would find all your attempts vain; there would be one or two open ends, place the hedges how you will; and then your field would not be encloſed, but open. Therefore BC muſt needs conſent to fall along EF; otherwiſe B being upon E, and C upon F, as I have already ſhewn you, BC muſt go on one ſide EF like one of the dotted lines; but then BC and EF, two ſtraight lines, would enclose a space, which the whole course of your experiments has shewn you, they cannot possibly do.

Then the triangles must exactly fall upon one another, &c.

I have been purposely prolix in this demonstration, to shew how it begins in experiment, goes on by experiment, and ends in an experimental conclusion. There may be another use in insisting so particularly upon the nature of the reasoning process here: among those who teach mathematics, without understanding their practical application, and also without entertaining a just idea of the nature of demonstration, there prevails a sort of pedantry productive of infinite disgust to the learner. If by detached figures I could shew the truth of any proposition in an instant, I am forbidden, because this is an *unmathematical* mode of proceeding; that

is,

is, mathematical reaſoning is ſuppoſed to be ſomething independent of experience, and the ſcience to be more refined than the experimental ſciences. Hence, if a Greek writer happens to have written a demonſtration a mile long, which demonſtration can be nothing but a concatenation of the reſults of obſervation and experiment, I muſt take this tedious round, rather than be allowed to arrive at the point deſired by only traverſing half a dozen yards, provided this ſhorter road leads through the unhallowed region of the ſenſes.

The fifth propoſition is ſaid to have ſtopped many ſtudents of geometry in their career; this is owing partly to the length of the demonſtration, and partly to the complication of the diagram. The demonſtration is, however, nothing but the reſult of the experiments in that of the fourth, combined with the reſult of two other very ſimple experiments; of which the one, that if you take equal parts from equal lines, the remainders ſhall be equal, will be eaſily granted from diſtinct recollection. The other, that if from equal angles you take equal parts, the remaining angels will be equal, ſhould be ſhewn by two pair of compaſſes, or two carpenter's rules opened equally, and then brought nearer together in both an equal and unequal degree. The reaſon why it becomes neceſſary to take pains to make beginners comprehend the nature of an angle, is becauſe in life we do not pay attention to the different expanſions of lines meeting at a point. On the contrary, there is not a child but what is accuſtomed to meaſure ſimple lengths.

I would rather chooſe to appeal to theſe two experiments, than to the third axiom placed before Euclid's elements, viz. that

if

if equals be taken from equals, the remainders will be equal. Mr. Locke has ſhewn the inſigniſicance of theſe axioms in the ſeventh chapter of his fourth book. In fact, they are only founded upon the induction of particular experiments and obſervations; and until that induction be compleat, we can never be convinced of their truth. They do not prove any thing themſelves, but require to be proved; and if a Newton were to devote his powers to the ſtudy of axioms for an hundred years, he would not be able to draw from them one ſingle concluſion worth notice.

In this manner does every demonſtration proceed upon the reſults of experiments, as the reader will find, in as many inſtances as he ſhall take the pains to examine. And ſince the appeal in demonſtrative reaſoning is always made to what is now exhibited to the ſenſes, or to what we have before learned by the exerciſe of the ſenſes, too much pains cannot be taken, at the commencement of the ſtudy of geometry, to satisfy the mind of the learner by appealing to his senses. The more distinct and deep the impressions of sense are at the beginning, the greater will the power of *abstraction* afterwards be, when the progress of his studies shall have carried him into the higher mathematics. *Abstraction* is not, in fact, a distinct *power*, as the metaphysicians, who seem to imagine that they increase the importance of their science, as they multiply distinctions, teach. We *abstract*, when we narrow the sphere of sensations and dwell upon impressions, or when we recollect the ideas thus acquired. So far is this talent from forming a distinction between man and beast, that the animals which do not take cognizance of more than two or three objects in this sublunary world may, I think, be fairly reckoned the most abstracted of all living creatures.—It is, at least, evident that of any object, I shall recollect the whole or *any part* the better, as the original impression was more lively. If I am to imagine, or *form an* *image*,

image, by putting things together in my mind, in an arrangement different from that in which I have beheld them, and thus create a whole which I have not feen, out of parts which I have feen; the diftinctnefs of the original conceptions will be equally fubfervient to this procefs. By appealing in this manner to his fenfes, and making him feel the firmnefs of the ground on which he treads, one might probably inftruct a boy, at an early age, in the elements of geometry, fo as rarely to give him difguft, and frequently great fatisfaction. He would by imperceptible degrees acquire the power of *abftraction*, or learn to reconfider each feparate perception, as well as to combine them anew.

Suppofing it unneceffary to multiply inftances of the experimental reafoning of geometry, fince the inftance already quoted fairly reprefents all the reft, I fhall fhortly con-

conſider the definitions of the firſt book of Euclid, except the merely nominal definitions, ſuch as thoſe of a rhomb, trapezium, &c.

There is, it ſeems, ſome uncertainty as to the author of the definitions. I ſhall take them, as they occur in Dr. Simſon's tranſlation, occaſionally, however, referring to Dr. Gregory's edition of the Greek text *.

DEFINITION I.

A point is that which hath no parts, or which hath no magnitude.

Σημειον ἐςἶι, ου μέρος ϰθεν.

Here the beginner immediately finds himſelf tranſported into the land of won-

* ΕΥΚΛΕΙΔΟΥ ΤΑ ΣΩΖΟΜΕΝΑ. Oxon. 1703. Ex Recenſione Davidis Gregorii, M. D.

ders;

ders; and ſuppoſing it neceſſary to his progreſs to conceive a thing that has no parts, he is apt to ſurmiſe that mathematics is a ſtudy for which nature never deſigned him; and as he proceeds, he looks back from time to time with an eye of regret upon the firſt definition, earneſtly wiſhing he had but force of mind enough to comprehend it. Dr. Simſon's demonſtration will not afford him any aſſiſtance in his difficulty; and he will ſtill be unable to conceive what that can be, which has no parts or magnitude; if a variety of phraſes be, as uſual, repeated to him; he may reply, it is in vain to utter new ſounds; what I want is ſenſible evidence of the thing; and if he ſhould but have the good fortune to attend to the evidence of his ſenſes, and to underſtand the nature of language, the difficulty will inſtantly vaniſh: for a point is firſt the end of any thing ſharp; *omne*

quod

quod pungit: then, by an eaſy derivation, any mark made by that ſharp thing; and this is the meaning of point in geometry. Perhaps the difficulty had never occurred, if inſtead of *point*, the word *dot*, or even *mark*, σημειον, had been always uſed in its place, and there had been no attempt at definition. For a point is only to mark the place whence a line is to begin, or where it is to end: γραμμῆς δὲ πέρατα σημεῖα. DEF. III. Thus in a circle it marks the ſpot within the figure, from which all ſtraight lines drawn to the circumference, are equal. Now one would make ſuch a mark as ſmall as poſſible, provided it be ſtill diſtinct, that the length of lines and their meetings and interſections may appear plainly, and from this effect of convenience has ariſen the phraſe that is ſuppoſed to deſcribe its eſſence; *that it is without parts.* This idea has nothing to do with the rea-

ſoning;

ſoning; all that is neceſſary is, that the *dot* or *mark* ſhould take up no ſenſible part of the line, in order that the diagram may be diſtinct. *Points* then are only ſubſervient to the convenience of conſtruction.

The next definition, after this explanation of the firſt, will preſent no difficulty.

DEFINITION II.

A line is length without breadth.

Γραμμη δε, μηκος απλατες.

Draw your lines as narrow as you conveniently can, your diagrams will be the clearer; but you cannot, and you need not, conceive length without breadth.

DEFINITION III.

The extremity of a line are points.

DEFINITION IV.

A ſtraight line is that which lies evenly between its extreme points.

Ευθεια γραμμη εϛιν, ἡτις εξισυ τοις εφ' εαυτης σημειοις κειται.

The impoſſibility of defining a word expreſſive of a ſimple perception is well known. The definition of a complex term conſiſts merely in the enumeration of the ſimple ideas, for which it ſtands. The only way of rendering the meaning of a ſimple term intelligible, is to exhibit the object of which it is the ſign; or, if you pleaſe, ſome ſenſible repreſentation of that object. A ſtraight line therefore muſt be ſhewn; and by drawing a crooked one at the ſame time, it will be perfectly underſtood, if any one require an explanation. All definitions muſt have ſome term, equally ly requiring a definition with that defined, as ἐξίσου, *evenly*, *upon an equality*.

The definitions of a ſurface, and a plane ſurface, muſt in like manner be made intelligible by an appeal to the ſenſes. By putting a ſtraight rule along different ſurfaces, it will appear whether they are plane or otherwiſe.

DEFINITION X.

When a ſtraight line ſtanding on another ſtraight line makes the adjacent angles equal to one another, each of the angles is called a right angle, and the line which ſtands on the other is called a perpendicular to it.

Here we have an appeal made to the ſenſes, which alone can inform us what is the expanſion between lines meeting at a point, or what is their inclination or bending towards each other. The eye can pretty well determine, whether the meeting lines are more inclined to each other on one ſide than the other, i. e. the equality or inequality of the adjacent angles. This meaſure of the eye would not be ſufficiently exact to ſatisfy us that the angles are equal; we muſt obtain a meaſure by real or imagined ſuper-poſition, as we do in one particular caſe, by applying the reſult of the demonſtration of the eighth, to the eleventh propoſition of Book I. But the term *right* probably preceded the application of any ſuch exact meaſure; and I ſhould conjecture, that it might be deduced from the meeting of lines or of bodies, that ſeemed to ſtand perfectly erect and not to bend towards each other; in the caſe of lines, ſtraight and right are perfectly ſynonymous; and an angle formed by the meeting of ſtraight lines, ſtanding right or upright, with reſpect to each other, would be be called a right angle: *linea recta, angulus rectus.* The application of the term *right*, would not, I ſuppoſe, be ſo obvious to certain angles formed by curved lines; yet it would be eaſily made, when men came to conſider ſuch angles, with a view to take their relative dimenſions accurately.

DEFINITION XV and XVI.

A circle is a plane figure contained by one line, which is called the circumference, and is ſuch, that all ſtraight lines drawn from a certain point, within the figure to the circumference, are equal to one another.

And this point is called the centre of the circle.

In theſe definitions, there is doubtleſs nothing embarraſſing. Yet for the ſake of perſons unaccuſtomed on the one hand to verbal analyſis, which forms a moſt important part of genuine *logic*, or the *theory of reaſoning*, it may not be improper to add the following remarks. An hoop, or any round object, eſpecially if hollow within, might ſupply the notion of a circle; but moſt probably a wheel with its ſpokes, and the central block of wood into which the interior extremities of the ſpokes are fixed, furniſhed the idea of the figure of the radii and centre; radius, we know, ſignifies a ſpoke: a ſignification previous, no doubt, to that of lines drawn from the centre to the circumference of a circle. All accurate ideas, founded upon meaſurement or careful compariſon, muſt neceſſarily be poſterior to approximations, ſuggeſted by a caſual or a diſtant ſurvey of objects; and a good deal of perplexity, when perſons firſt engage in the ſtudy of mathematics, ariſes from the reſult of vague obſervations,

ſervations, mixing itſelf with the reſult of the exact experiments employed in the reaſoning of mathematics.

Centre is ſimply *a point*, *a dot*, *a mark*, ſhewing the common origin of the radii. This is the ſecondary ſignification of the ſubſtantive κεντρον, derived from the verb κεντεω *pungo*, *ſtimulo*, provided the etymologiſts of Holland have not reverſed the natural order of derivation, and I ſhall hereafter endeavour to render it probable, from ſome very ſimple conſiderations, and even from data which they themſelves afford, that they have. Their reſearches, however, even ſo, retain a great value. In theſe caſes, the beſt ſervice a perſon can render to letters, next to writing the truth, is to write exactly the reverſe.—At all events, the firſt ſignification of κεντρον, is a *goad*, or any thing ending in a ſharp point; and hence the mark left by preſſing this point againſt any yielding ſurface. If a man were to begin to ſtudy geometry, independently of all ideas of viſion, he muſt have the points whence lines are to be drawn, the centre of a circle, &c. marked by ſome ſharp projecting point or a ſmall hollow.

In Lennep's Etymologicum, we have the following account of the origin of κιρκος and κυκλος.

Κιρκος, *circus* (item *circulus*, et *annulus*) ortum eſt a κίρω, quod vicinum verbo κειρω. Communis autem origo eſt κεω, κιω, cujus *propria* notio poſita eſt in *motu*, qui fit *impellendo allidendove*. Et κιρω quidem vicinum videtur verbo γυρω, cujus origo γυω. Eâdem autem ratione, ut a γυρω ortum γῦρος, ſignificat motum rei in ſe redeuntis, ſic noſtrum κιρκος circum ſignificare videtur.—Again, κυκλος, cyclus, circus . . . . . .

repeten-

repetendum eſt a *κυλιω*, vel formâ quâdam vicina, id autem eſt *volvo*.

The *poſtulates* prefixed to Euclid's Elements, preſent themſelves in a form of which, perhaps, Mr. Ludlam felt the awkwardneſs, when he obſerved, "that the "poſtulates are not to be ſo underſtood, as "if Euclid required a practical dexterity "in managing a ruler and pencil. They "are here ſet down, that his reader may "admit the *poſſibility* of what he may here-"after require to be done. To ſhew that "what he thus requires contains no ab-"ſurdity, no repugnant ideas, Euclid in "the courſe of a demonſtration, requires "you to produce a terminated ſtraight line. "Was this as impoſſible in idea, as it is to "take a greater number out of a leſs, the "whole demonſtration muſt fail; for the "ſteps of a demonſtration, like the links "of a chain, hang by one another; Eu-"clid,

" clid, therefore, in this place, enumerates " all the operations required in his future " demonſtrations and problems; requiring " their poſſibility to be here acknowledged, " and thus precludes all future objections " on this head." (*Rudiments, Ed. 3d. p.* 137.) Theſe poſtulates were, indeed, probably introduced by cavils, or the dread of cavils: but if that which is demanded had been denied, the author would have been ſo thoroughly convinced by his ſenſes, that he could produce a ſtraight line to any requiſite diſtance, or deſcribe a circle with any radius, that he would have gone on with perfect aſſurance in his reaſoning. Should any one object to a demonſtration, " but how am I ſure that theſe things are " true, of lines reaching from the earth to " the moon, or of a circle that ſhould be " deſcribed from the ſun as a centre, and " at the diſtance of Sirius?" It is impoſſible

ſible to convince ſuch an objector, by direct ſenſible teſtimony, or rather it is impoſſible to make him own a conviction, which we are ſure he muſt feel. It is then idle to clog an elementary book with forms or matter intended to obviate ſuch objections. All that ſhould be inſerted, is juſt enough to ſatisfy a perſon, that will, *bonâ fide*, make uſe of his faculties.

Moſt of the AXIOMS were probably introduced, in conſequence of that perverſion of the human underſtanding, which the ſtudy of *generals* occaſioned. " The rules " eſtabliſhed in the ſchools, ſays Mr. " Locke, that all reaſonings are *ex præ-* " *cognitis et præconceſſis*, ſeem to lay the " foundation of all other knowledge in " theſe maxims, and to ſuppoſe them to be " *præcognita*, whereby, I think, are meant " theſe two things, firſt, that theſe axioms " are thoſe truths that are firſt known to " the

" the mind; and ſecondly, that upon them " the other parts of our knowledge de- " pend." (B. iv. c. 7. §. 8.) He goes on to ſhew, 1. That theſe axioms are not the truths firſt known; and, 2. That the other parts of our knowledge do not depend upon them; and then challenges any ſcholaſtic man, to lay before him the whole frame and ſyſtem of any ſcience ſo built upon axioms, that they cannot be ſhewn to ſtand as firmly without any conſideration of them. Theſe axioms then ought to be expunged from books of geometry; 1. as unneceſſary; and, 2. as tending to give the beginner wrong notions of the foundation of knowledge, and the means by which we render ourſelves certain in any caſe of doubt. Conſidering what commentaries we have lately had from no deſpicable hands upon the *verités premiéres* of Pere Buffier, it is not yet ſuperfluous to apprize the

the ſtudent where human knowledge begins, and how certainty is acquired.

In the 35th definition, and the 12th *axiom*, as it is improperly called, we have expreſſed the reſult of our common obſervation of parallel lines. This part of Euclid has been the occaſion of infinite but needleſs perplexity to editors and commentators. Had they been aware of the nature of geometrical reaſoning, they would have entertained leſs anxiety on account of the foundation upon which the doctrine of parallel lines is to be built; for it is remarkable, that though all, as far as I know, from Savile to Ludlam, object to Euclid, and each propoſes an aſſumption at ſetting out different from that of his predeceſſors, yet all are perfectly ſatisfied with the concluſions; and there never probably was a perſon, who after paying proper attention, doubted of the truth of the 27th,

28th,

28th, 29th, or 30th proposition of the first book of Euclid, or of the most remote consequence deduced from them. The fact is, the senses give decisive evidence of these properties. All the difference in the projects for correcting Euclid's method consists in this, that one writer proposes to set out from one result, another from another; all of them true, and more or less obvious. Dr. Austin proposes to set out from the equality of the alternate angles; a fact more remote from immediate inspection, than any of the others; but even to this method there can be no objection, provided the pupil be shewn, that this equality does actually exist. Other writers begin with properties less remote from vulgar observation. Dr. Simson proposes these *axioms*, "a straight line cannot first go nearer to another straight line and then go further from it, before it cuts it, nor recede,

recede, and then approach, nor keep the ſame diſtance .or a part of its courſe, and then recede or approach;" that is, in ſhorter and clearer terms, that a ſtraight is not a crooked or a bent line; as for inſtance, in

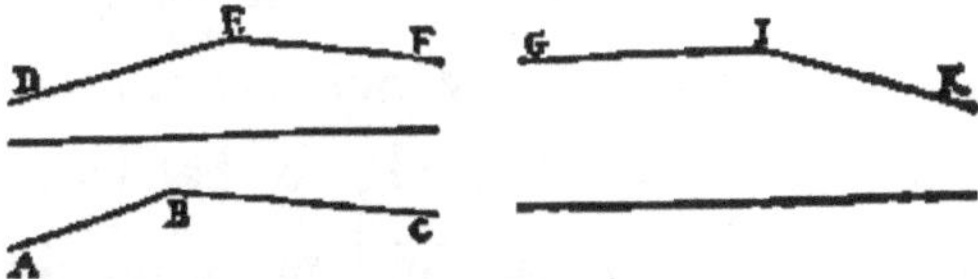

the lines above, that a ſtraight line can never take the direction of ABC, or DEF, or GIK: he afterwards goes through five tireſome demonſtrations, as if the elements of Euclid were not already tedious enough.

Mr. Ludlam, as we ſhall preſently ſee, propoſes a ſhorter, and therefore a better way, to demonſtrate the 29th propoſition.

A very ſimple reflection will make it appear, why ſo many different facts have been ſuggeſted as the foundation of propoſitions concerning parallel lines. We do

not

not uſually in the courſe of life; treaſure up any exact reſult upon this ſubject; nor can we ſatisfy ourſelves here, by bringing one figure and laying it upon another, or meaſuring it in any very ſimple way, as in the experiments upon which the reaſoning has been hitherto founded; ſo that we can have no fundamental facts quite familiar, nor altogether ſo ſimple, as thoſe upon which we have hitherto proceeded; but the want of familiarity, the fruit of paſt obſervation, may be eaſily made up by preſent attention; of a truth of which the ſenſes are perfectly equal to take cognizance, we ſhall, after due attention, feel the ſame conviction, whether we happen to find it out ourſelves or have it pointed out to us. And the reaſoning concerning parallel lines, though neither beginning in ideas ſo ſimple or ſo familiar, will nevertheleſs prove equally concluſive with the reaſoning that has gone before.

On an hundred different occaſions, in our playful and in our ſerious moods, we have obſerved the coincidence of ſtraight lines, and meaſured lengths; our obſervation of ruts traced by wheel carriages, as alſo of frame-work in which bars are laid alongſide of each other, gives us a diſtinct idea of ſtraight lines that perpetually preſerve the ſame diſtance: and we ſhall find alſo upon calling to mind our paſt obſervations, and holding them ſteadily in view, that if lines do not preſerve the ſame diſtance, they muſt, if produced far enough, at laſt meet on one ſide or other of a ſtraight line, which croſſes them, let them converge ever ſo ſlowly *.

The

* *Parallel ſtraight lines are ſuch as are in the ſame plane, and which being produced ever ſo far both ways do* *not*

The truth of the reſult, expreſſed in Euclid's 12th *axiom*, as it is ſo improperly called,

not meet. Thus the 35th definition ſtands in Simſon's Euclid. It has been objected to, "as a vulgar and "inaccurate conception, containing no given finite "quantity, and furniſhing no meaſure or ſtandard, "from which an equation might be made; and that "nothing could be expected from ſuch a definition in "a ſcience, *all* whoſe axioms expreſs only equati-"ons." (Auſtin's Examination of Euclid, p. 13.) This definition may, in one ſenſe, be regarded as a verbal definition, an explanation of the word *parallel*; which word need not be uſed in the elements of geometry, juſt as for triangle we might always uſe the phraſe, *a plane figure contained by three ſtraight lines*. Thus in the enunciation of propoſition the 29th, we might ſay, *if a ſtraight line, falling upon two other ſtraight lines, makes the alternate angles equal to one another; theſe two ſtraight lines*, being produced ever ſo far both ways, ſhall never meet, inſtead of, *ſhall be parallel*.

The 10th axiom in Simſon, proves Dr. A's concluding remark not to be juſt. Moreover, it appears to me that the called, may be clearly ſhewn by the following experiment, and he may have in-

the idea of lines that never meet, is one of the cleareſt and moſt ſatisfactory the ſenſes bring to the mind; and it is, beſides, abundantly ſimple. But, in order to remove all uncertainty, if the caſual obſervations from which the term *parallelifm* is derived, ſhould have left any, fix two pencils at a convenient diſtance in a piece of wood; let one end of this piece of wood be terminated in a plane, large enough to keep true to the face of a ruler. By this ſimple apparatus, a child at a very early age, might be convinced, that lines traced by theſe pencils, would never meet, ſince they muſt always have the ſame diſtance between them, as long as the pencils continue to be moved along the face of the ruler. And in this manner we ſhall have an experimental proof of the above 27th propoſition, againſt which the cavil of Proclus will not be able to raiſe a ſcruple.—The difficulties, in ſhort, that have been propoſed on the ſubject of parallel lines, and the contrivances to obviate them, equally evince the experimental nature of mathematical reaſoning.

ferred it either from ſome ſuch experiment made or imagined; or from knowing, that the angles of a plane triangle are equal to two right angles. The *axiom* is; "if a "ſtraight meets two ſtraight lines, ſo as to "make the two interior angles on the ſame "ſide of it taken together leſs than two "right angles, theſe ſtraight lines being "continually produced, ſhall at length "meet upon that ſide on which are the "angles which are leſs than two right "angles."

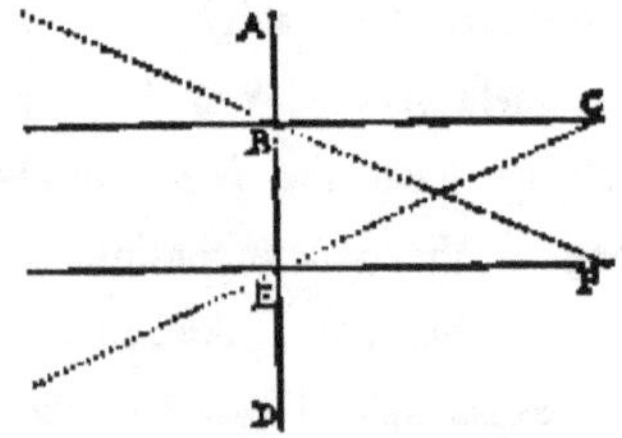

Let a ſtraight line ſo fall upon two other ſtraight lines, that the angles ABC and CBD, are equal to one another, and alſo the

the angles AEF and FED, (which may be done either by experiment or by former propoſitions) then the lines CB and FE ſtand upright with reſpect to AD, or the angles, being adjacent and equal, are right angles according to the definition. Now in a model conſtructed according to this diagram, let CB, or EF, or both, be moveable, or have a joint at B and E, then by turning either of them inwards, or in the direction of the dotted lines EC or BF, they will meet and form a triangle, if produced. So that if theſe angles, which by the conſtruction are equal to two right angles, become at all leſs, *the ſtraight lines, continually produced, ſhall at length meet upon that ſide, on which are the angles which are leſs than two right angles*; which was to be ſhewn.

The following experiments would furniſh a ſatisfactory demonſtration of the lead-ing properties of parallel lines; let parallel lines be ſhewn to be ſuch as always to preſerve the ſame diſtance; hence all the ſtraight lines meeting them internally at equal angles ſhall be equal. Thus let AB be a ſtraight

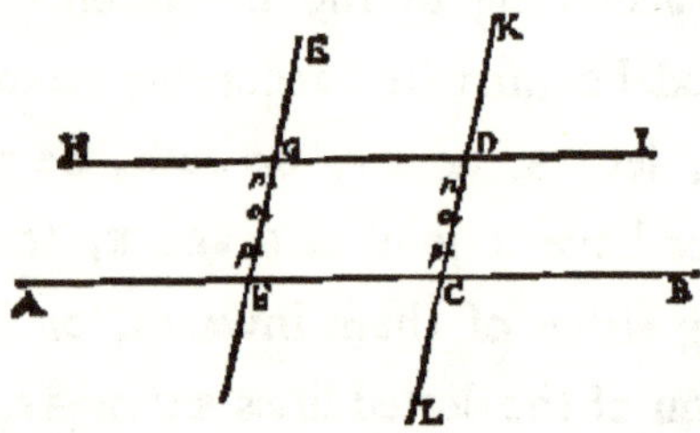

line; and let DC make with it the angle DCB. At the point F make the angle GFB equal to DCB, and the line FG equal to DC, and through G and D draw the line HI. Now the angles DCB and GFB being equal, and GF equal to DC, the lines AB and HI are parallel. Now let us ſuppoſe a model made according to this diagram, ſo that the line HI might move along GF and DC, upon each of which certain ſmall equal

diſtances

diſtances are marked off, as *n*, *o*, *p*. It is evident, that if HI were brought down through theſe equal ſmall diſtances ſucceſſively, it would be parallel, for F*n* is equal to C*n*, and ſo on; and at laſt it would coincide with AB, and not cut it. Therefore, the internal angle DCB is equal to the external, and oppoſite KDI, (ſuppoſing DC to be prolonged to K) becauſe they would be the ſame angle; and the alternate angles GDC, DCB, would be equal, as being now the vertical angles DCB and FCL; and the interior angles, IDC coinciding with BCL and BCD with IDK, would, by propoſition the 13th, be equal to two right angles; and any line parallel to AB would be parallel to HI, prop. 30th. On ſeparating the ſtraight ſtrips again, it would appear, that if the alternate angles be equal, the exterior equal to the interior and oppoſite, and both interior equal to two right angles, the lines would keep parallel, and if any of these circumſtances change, the angles would not be parallel, for the lines forming the equal angles, would become unequal.

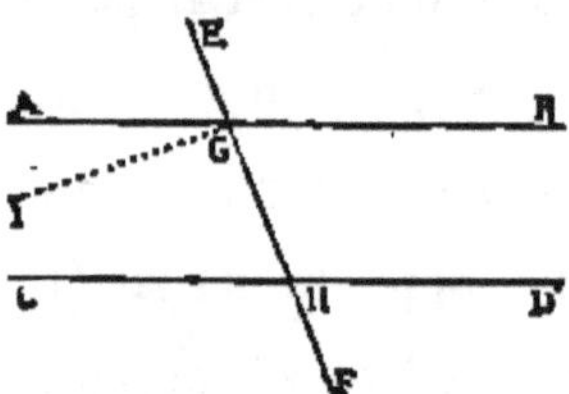

A courſe of experiments on parallel lines may begin in a manner different ſtill. Mr. Ludlam propoſes to demonſtrate the equality of the alternate angles, for which alone the 12th *axiom* is needed, by the following experiment, which he miſcalls an axiom. *Two ſtraight lines, meeting in a point, are not* BOTH *parallel to a third line.* For, ſays he, if AGH be not equal to GHD (the alternate angle) one muſt be greater; let

AGH

AGH be the greater. At the point G, make IGH equal to GHD, (by prop. 23. I.) then IG is parallel to CD by 27. I. But by ſupp. AG is alſo parallel to CD, therefore AG and IG, meeting in a point at G, are both parallel to CD, which is impoſſible by the axiom, (i. e. it will be found ſo upon trial.) *Rudim*, p. 144.

This is perfectly ſatisfactory. In a word, when we come to reflect upon our perceptions, we diſcover a conſtant equality of diſtance, or the impoſſibility of their meeting to be a character of parallel lines; but this is not ſufficient, for we muſt have a meaſure of this equality; and by continuing our attention a ſtep further, we perceive that this meaſure may be either the equality of lines making equal interior angles with one of the parallel lines, or what is a particular caſe of the ſame reſult, the equality of lines falling at right angles upon the

the infide of parallel lines. I have no other reafon for preferring either of thefe meafures, than that it feems to be the firft accurate refult we arrive at in confidering parallel lines. Any other clear inference from manual or mental experiments, will afford an equally firm bafe for the reafoning; and any of the firft properties attributed by Euclid to parallel lines, may be employed for this purpofe. They are all about equally diftant from our previous knowledge, and all may with nearly equal eafe, be proved by experiment. In Euclid's Elements, the truth feems to me to be fo frequently obfcured by demonftration, and fo much difguft is often excited by his tedious method of proceeding, that were it not a violation of that loyalty which we owe to our mafters, the Greeks, I wifh the fhorteft poffible method might be followed in teaching the rudiments of mathematics

matics by the help of ſimple ſatisfactory experiments. And if there be any one who ſhould have learned geometry in this way, let him be aſſured that he holds his proficiency by a firm tenure. In this ſcience there is no tranſcendental road; but I imagine a *royal* road might be ſtruck out, though Euclid was of a different opinion. The ſooner too we quit the geometrical for the algebraic method, the better. Not only has algebra all the general advantages aſcribed to the ſtudy of mathematics, by Bacon and Locke, but one peculiar to itſelf. Not only "if the wit be dull, does "the analytic method ſharpen it; if too "wandering, fix it; if too inherent in the "ſenſe, abſtract it;" but it confers the power of invention and combination beyond any other ſtudy; in geometry indeed, compared with algebra, the mind may be ſaid to be paſſive. The power of readily calling

calling up poſſibilities before the imagination, of contraſting them with realities and with one another, and of deciding on their reſpective merits, appears to me the higheſt ſtate of perfection, at which our faculties can arrive. A perſon, poſſeſſed of this talent, is prepared equally to excel in thought and conduct; and the reſources of his mind will be inexhauſtible. Now an acute obſervation, and juſt conception of things actual, joined to an habit of comparing and combining them, not unlike that caſting about of the thoughts which takes place in the ſolution of algebraic problems, is the only way, I believe, in which this ineſtimable talent can be acquired.

Should it be objected, that if we appeal as directly as poſſible to the ſenſes in teaching the elements of geometry, we ſhall impair the power of abſtraction, I anſwer, that this method will confer the power

of

of abſtraction in a ſuperior degree. The ſenſes will deliver more diſtinct ideas to the memory; and the more firmly the memory holds ideas, the more eaſily will the imagination and the judgment be enabled to perform their functions. Natural ſuperiority of intellect can ariſe only from an happier organization of the ſenſes, or the *ſenſorium* *. Now by exerciſing the ſenſes pro-

* Hence the long agitated queſtion concerning original determination, or innate diſpoſition, towards any particular purſuit, may be decided with perfect preciſion. That the ſmalleſt tendency towards mathematics, poetry, &c. exiſts at the time of birth, is a chimæra too abſurd to be ſeriouſly combated now. It is ſufficient to obſerve an infant, or to be acquainted with the origin of ideas, to diſmiſs from the mind this ſuggeſtion of ignorance and indolence. Beſides, why are not geniuſes for arts or ſciences born among ſavages, as frequently as in nations where theſe arts and ſciences flouriſh? If theſe germs of particular talents pre-exiſt

properly during the firſt period of life, we may make up, by continued attention, for their deficiency of original acuteneſs. And where nature has beſtowed her nobleſt gifts, ſuperior powers of perception, retention, and combination, we ſhall thus turn them to the beſt poſſible advantage.

Should

exiſt in the mind, we might expect to ſee them occaſionally vegetate, and at length produce fruit, independently of the ſtate of ſociety; but we ſee evidently, that particular eminence is always engrafted upon general talents, often at a late period in life, and in no caſe the ſpontaneous produce of the intellect.—A peculiar organization, however, may be conſidered in one ſenſe as an original determination towards a particular purſuit. Thus a peculiar organization of the ear, which perhaps experiment would ſhew to be only a quicker ſenſe of hearing, and ſo to differ in degree, not in kind, diſpoſes to inſtrumental muſic: A good ear with an agreeable voice to vocal muſic alſo. A well-organized and very pliant hand may determine to occupations

cupations

Should theſe reflections be juſt, and ſhould it alſo be admitted, that in demonſtrative reaſoning, we proceed purely by experiments, as will, I hope, hardly now be doubted; it would be advantageous, in order to beſtow the habit of obſerving with attention, to conſtruct a geometrical ap-

cupations requiring manual dexterity. In powers of vociſeration a man, to the annoyance of his neighbours, often feels a vocation to become an orator.—The relative ſtructure of the organ, by which we combine ideas, ſeems to be in every reſpect independent of thoſe by which we receive them. Though the eye or ear be well or ill organized, it does not follow that the brain ſhall be well or ill organized. And to the combining as well as the retaining faculty, it ſeems perfectly indifferent, what ſort of ideas it has preſented to it; whether of ſounds, colours, mathematical, poetical, or any other. Except therefore thoſe purſuits, which are immediately connected with external organization, we cannot be ſaid, in any ſenſe whatever, to receive from nature any particular determination.

paratus, which might be employed in the early part of education. Should ſuch an apparatus be preſented to children, without any of the forbidding airs of pedantry, I imagine that in this mode of ſtudying geometry, they would find no leſs relief than improvement; they would find at leaſt employment for their ſenſes; and every thing we can obſerve in children, conſpires with every thing we know of the human underſtanding, to ſhew that nature intended us during the firſt period of life, to be chiefly employed in exerciſing them. The ſoul of a child, (from his earlieſt infancy, when he will always, while awake, be obſerved to be collecting ideas, by his hands and eyes in particular,) may be ſaid eſſentially to reſide in his ſenſes. At a riper age the combination of theſe ideas engages a conſiderable ſhare of attention; and at an advanced age, when the ſenſes are blunted, the exercise of the internal faculties will still more occupy a mind previously well stored.

But according to the modern practice of education, instead of suffering children to follow the active tendency of their nature, or gently directing it, we forcibly debar them from the exercise of the senses, and condemn them to the horrible drudgery of learning by rote, the conceits of a tribe of sophists and semi-barbarians, to whom it is no reproach not to have entertained just ideas either concerning words or things. Next to actual blind-folding and muffling, to oblige children to learn the terms in which these conceits are couched, is the happiest contrivance imaginable, for keeping their minds unfurnished; by long continuance of sedentary confinement, we hold the perceptive faculties, as much as possible, in a state of perfect inaction; at the ſame time we employ the organs of ſpeech in pronouncing, and the memory in retaining, none but ſounds inſignificant; ſo that from the commencement of a liberal education, one might be led to conclude, that the following is the only ſentence, ever written by Mr. Locke, of which his countrymen have attempted an application; "if it were "worth while, no doubt a child might be "ſo ordered, as to have but a very few, "even of the ordinary ideas, till he were "grown up to a man;" and that nothing might be wanting to ſatisfy us, that our apparent cruelty is *real kindneſs*, it has been clearly proved, that the principal rules laid down in our grammars are falſe, and the exceptions groundleſs! Let the moraliſt, when he has verified this fact in the writings of Mr. Tooke, and his fellow labourers in the philoſophy of language, determine whether it be an act of

greater

greater humanity, to preſerve the Africans from ſlavery, or deliver children from *grammar* *.

The

* Thanks to Mrs. BARBAULD, who has entitled herſelf to the everlaſting gratitude of parents and children, one great point in education has already been gained: as long as the ſuperintendance of the mother laſts, books calculated to improve them in every reſpect, are now commonly put into the hands of children. Theſe books are equally intelligible and amuſing.

But no ſooner have the boys croſſed the threſhold of the grammar ſchool, than they experience the moſt dreadful reverſe. And during a great part of their continuance at ſchool, they are ſubjected to the moſt exquiſite mental torture that can well be deviſed. The following untranſlatable character, by Valckenaer, (*Obſerv. ad Orig. Græc. p.* 4.) may ſerve to ſhew how much boys are likely to ſuffer, and how much to gain, while they are toiling through their Greek grammar: and no one will accuſe Valckenaer of rating the knowledge of the Greek language below its value.—" Recentiorum *grammaticæ*, ut vocantur, *Græcæ* ad prima linguæ rudimenta facili methodo diſcenda vix ac ne vix

 quidem

The illuſtrations already given, would, I preſume, enable the moſt inexperienced reader in other caſes, to diſcern the reſults of experiment upon which mathematical reaſoning muſt always proceed. But ſo

quidem accommodatæ, REGULIS INEPTIS, TORTUOSIS ANOMALIARUM TRICIS, ET VANORUM AC NUGANTIUM HOMINUM SPINOSIS DELIRAMENTIS ſunt refertiſſimæ." Our Latin grammars are, I preſume, little leſs plentifully provided than our Greek with FALSE AND FOOLISH RULES, PERPLEXING EXCEPTIONS AND THE DISGUSTING RAVINGS OF VAIN AND EMPTY TRIFLERS. I, who believe in the impreſcriptible right of boys and girls to a good education, think parents in conſcience bound to exert themſelves ſtrenuouſly, in order that children be taught ſomething very different from theſe odious ſubtleties. One thing they may reckon upon as certain, that though occaſionally a degree of attention may be requiſite beyond what a child will chearfully beſtow, yet if education goes on, upon the whole, unpleaſantly, it is ill-conducted. Children commonly acquire *ideas* with pleaſure, and pride themſelves in the acquiſition.

much

much has been written concerning the 5th definition of the 5th book, that I may be permitted to add a few obſervations upon this particular difficulty. The terms of this definition ſo exactly reſemble the terms in which "*every curious noſtrum and choice* "*receipt*" is delivered, that one may wonder how Mr. Harris himſelf could fail to perceive, in this inſtance at leaſt, that mathematical reaſoning is founded upon experiment or experience, which, as he juſtly obſerves, is no more than "the reſult of many repeated experiments." The firſt of four magnitudes, we are told in this definition, has the ſame ratio to the ſecond, that the third has to the fourth, when any equimultiples of the firſt and third *being taken*, and any equimultiples whatever of the ſecond and fourth, if when the multiple of the firſt is leſs than that of the ſecond, the multiple of the third is leſs than the multiple of the fourth, if when equal, equal; and if when greater, greater. I know not how it is poſſible more directly to appeal to experiment, than firſt to tell us to double certain magnitudes upon themſelves as often as we pleaſe, and then to obſerve whether the firſt and third having been ſo doubled upon themſelves an equal number of times reſpectively, exceed or equal the ſecond and fourth treated in the ſame manner, or fall ſhort of them.

Euclid's definition is doubtleſs embarraſſing; beginners do not eaſily catch the ſenſe; beſides the new terms it contains, and the neceſſity it impoſes of transferring the attention to alternate magnitudes, it involves another conſiderable difficulty. It expreſſes a reſult which ſcarce any beginner will be able to draw from the review of his experience. And yet it is abſolutely neceſſary, that before he proceeds, he

ſhould

ſhould be ſatisfied of its truth. It has been idly obſerved, that though no ſuch thing as a circle or ſtraight line ſhould exiſt, our reaſoning concerning them would be equally valid. But did not our ſenſes apprize us of their exiſtence, and enable us to diſcover their properties, it is very certain that we ſhould never have reaſoned at all concerning them. Every *definition*, as they are perhaps not happily termed, either expreſſes an object that lies immediately within the ſphere, and can be recognized by a ſingle application, of the ſenſes; or elſe a reſult which requires ſeveral ſucceſſive applications of the ſenſes. In the firſt caſe the object, if not already well known, muſt be exhibited; in the ſecond, we muſt make ſucceſſive appeals to the ſenſes. In order " to underſtand Euclid's fifth definition, ſays Mr. Ludlam, inſtances of its applica-

 tion

tion in particular cafes muft be given *." The refult, defcribed in the definition, was probably deduced by its author from a train of mental experiments, which he omitted to fet down, as Sir Ifaac Newton has fometimes done. Every commentator has laboured to fupply thefe reflections or experiments. And this muft be done by the teacher, for there will be few beginners fagacious enough to deduce it for themfelves.

* P. 167. In another paffage, however, the fame author fets out with this grofs miftake. "The bufi-" nefs of fcience, fays he, is from a few general prin-" ciples, to draw a great number of particular con-" clufions." Mr. Ludlam's book having, in the courfe of a few years, come to a third edition, muft have been put into the hands of many young people; and one may, on this account, lament the more that his notions are fo confufed as they often appear to be.

The difficulty may be eaſily overcome: let us recollect, that the only way of explaining words denoting ſimple perceptions, is to excite thoſe ſimple perceptions; and again, that the only way of explaining general terms, is to enumerate the ſigns of thoſe ſimple perceptions which the general term comprehends; and then, if neceſſary, to explain the ſimple terms, by ſhewing the correſponding objects. Now *proportion* ſignifies a ſeries of ſimple perceptions. Upon applying a meaſure to two diſtant objects, and finding one to be ten times as tall as the other, we ſay that the height of A has to that of B, the proportion of ten to one; and with reſpect to height, we conſider B as the tenth *portion* of A. But proportion is uſed to expreſs a more indirect and complicated compariſon of quantities, when we can neither bring them together, nor meaſure them ſeparately. Thus

Thus when of two perſons varying in ſize and ſtature, I ſay of one (A) that he is as fat as another (B), I may not mean that the weight of A's fat equals the weight of B's fat: but that if the bones and muſcles of A are half as heavy as the bones and muſcles of B, the fat of A ſhall be half as heavy as that of B. If Britain among eight millions of inhabitants, have 200 perſons eminent in ſcience and letters; and France, with 25 millions of inhabitants, have 625 perſons equally eminent in ſcience and letters, then the Engliſh, you would ſay, is as learned and ſcientific a nation as the French. And for the reſult of this indirect kind of compariſon, we uſe the term *proportion* *: and

* For want of being acquainted with the analyſis of terms, which indeed in the extent to which it has been lately carried, may be conſidered as a new ſpecies of knowledge, Dr. Price, I think, has maintained, that the

and whenever we find four magnitudes, of which we perceive one to be exactly as great, when compared with the second, as the third is when compared to the fourth, we express this observation, by saying, that the first has to the second, the same ratio that the third has to the fourth. With respect to numbers, when according to Euclid's

the idea of proportion is derived from the understanding, and not from the senses. He might as well have maintained, that the ideas of *a*, *b*, *c*, as used in algebraic equations, are derived from the understanding, and not the senses. Abstract terms partake very much of the nature of algebraic terms, and if Dr. Price had happened to view them in this light, he must have seen his error. The highest and most perfect abstraction is exhibited in the terms of algebra. To many abstract words of common language, somewhat of their individual corporeal signification adheres; and even when this is quite lost, they can only represent a certain sort or number of ideas, which being in frequent

Euclid's 20th definition of book the 7th, the firſt number is the ſame multiple, or part of the ſecond, as the third is of the fourth; we ſay, that the firſt bears the ſame proportion to the ſecond, that the third bears to the fourth. In making experiments upon any four magnitudes, of which we perceive the firſt to be exactly as great, when compared to the ſecond, as the third compared to the fourth; we ſhall

quent demand, it is convenient to have ready bundled up for exchange in converſation, to ſave the trouble of counting them out, one by one. In algebra the ſigns are arbitrary; and hence their force is perfectly clear. The ſenſe is not obſcured by the intruſion of any collateral ſignification, nor do we pre-ſuppoſe that knowledge of the import of the terms, which often with reſpect to complex terms, does not exiſt, but aſſign it preciſely beforehand.

Mr. Ludlam informs his readers, "that the idea of ratio is a ſimple idea," p. 166. Such is his apprehenſion of the nature of terms.

find

find, that when we double the firſt and third upon themſelves any equal number of times, they will for ever be reſpectively as great, when compared to the ſecond and fourth, either remaining as at firſt, or alſo doubled upon themſelves any equal number of times; ſo that having clearly conceived this by the help of trials upon various magnitudes, we ſhall be aſſured, that if the firſt and third of four magnitudes, be taken any equal number of times, and the magnitudes thence reſulting ſhall not be exactly as great, when reſpectively compared to the ſecond and fourth, or their equimultiples, the one as the other, then the original four magnitudes cannot have been exactly as great, the firſt compared to the ſecond, as the third compared to the fourth. From this conſtant correſpondence in the increaſe of proportional magnitudes, it will appear, upon due conſideration, that what-

ever

ever equimultiples be taken as aforesaid, the first multiple will be, when compared with the second, what the third is when compared with the fourth *.

Con-

* Under the title of "*A Demonstration of the 5th Def. B. V. of Euclid,*" Mr. Robertson, public Lecturer in Geometry at Oxford, has proved by a very ingenious train of experiments, the truth of the result assumed by Euclid. He shews, that if we have four magnitudes, the first being to the second as the third to a magnitude less than the fourth, (for instance, 6, 4, 9, 7,) then it is possible to take certain equimultiples of the first and third, and certain equimultiples of the second and fourth, such, that the multiple of the first shall be greater than that of the second, but the multiple of the third not greater than that of the fourth. Thus:

$(6\times6=)\ 36\ (8\times4=)\ 32\ (6\times9=)\ 54\ (8\times7=)\ 56;$

Again he shews, that if the first be to the second, as the third is to a magnitude greater than the fourth, then certain equimultiples can be taken of the first and third, and certain equimultiples of the second and fourth;

Concerning the language uſed in deſcribing proportion, there prevails an erroneous notion. Sir Iſaac Newton has tranſmitted it to the writers of compendiums of mathematics and natural philoſophy; it reſpects

fourth; ſuch, that the multiple of the firſt ſhall be leſs than the multiple of the ſecond, but the multiple of the third not leſs than the multiple of the fourth. Thus, to illuſtrate the ſenſe of this propoſition alſo, by an arithmetical example, take 6, 4, 9, 5, and repeat the alternate numbers the ſame number of times.

Let (6×3=) 18 (4×5=) 20 (9×3=) 27 (5×5=) 25; the magnitudes, being doubled upon themſelves, increaſe ſo, that when the 4th is leſs when compared with the 3d, than the 2d when compared with the 1ſt, the multiple of the 2d comes to exceed or equal that of the 1ſt, when that of the 4th is leſs than that of the 3d, and *v. v.* when the 4th is greater compared the 3d, than the 2d with the 1ſt.

By taking different pieces of tape, of which the 4th is made firſt greater and then leſs, when compared to the 3d, than the 2d when compared to the 1ſt; a boy ſpects the meaning of the word AS. The truth is, AS has no peculiar ſignification as has generally been aſſerted after him. It may always be exchanged for *it*, *that*, *what*, or, *that which*, alike in common and philoſophical diſcourſe. Thus, *New-*

will ſoon perceive, that by being doubled itſelf, while the reſt are alſo doubled upon themſelves in the manner directed by Euclid; this 4th will be at ſome period of its multiplication, equal to the 3d, or leſs, or greater, when the multiple of the 2d is not equal, or greater, or leſs, than that of the firſt. By this exerciſe he will catch the point of view, under which to conſider the proportion of magnitudes accurately. The appearance of abſtruſeneſs, which is ſo repulſive to beginners, ariſes ſolely from their having been unaccuſtomed to compare magnitudes with attention in this way. The idea of teaching the elements of geometry by lengths of tape, may ſeem ridiculous; but I ſuſpect, that thoſe who are accuſtomed to give inſtruction in this part of the ſcience, are not entitled by their experience of the ſucceſs of the uſual method to be ſcornful.

ton is to other philoſophers, as Homer is to other poets; or what *Homer is to other poets, Newton is to other philoſophers, viz. the greateſt of all.* So in ſtating proportions, as 3 is to 4, as 9 is to 12, or 3 is to 4, what 9 is to 12; and A is to B inverſely or reciprocally, *what* C is to D; and *as* or *what* ſhortly expreſs *as much greater or leſs than,* or *equal to.* See the Επεα πτερ. p. 283, and the following pages, where the article or conjunction *as*, is ſo far explained, though its original *corporeal* ſenſe is not given.

III.

Mr. Locke defines *knowledge* to be *the perception of the connexion and agreement, or diſagreement and repugnancy, of any of our ideas.* In this alone, ſays he, it conſiſts. "Where this perception is, there is knowledge; and where it is not, there, though we may fancy, guefs or believe, yet we always come fhort of knowledge; for, when we know that *white is not black*, what do we elfe than perceive, that thefe two ideas do not agree?" He goes on, through the firft chapter of his fourth book, to illuftrate his definition. But his definition appears to me far from happy, and his commentary far from fatisfactory. It would perhaps have fpared him fome unneceffary words and vain diftinctions, if, as knowledge arifes from the perceptions of fenfe, he had made it to confift in the confcioufnefs of thofe perceptions; but I fufpect his favourite example of the equality of the three angles of a triangle to two right angles, which he alfo produces upon this occafion, led him to adopt expreffions not fufficiently comprehenfive. When he obferved, B. II. ch. 1. §. 19. that "it is the "affectation of knowing *beyond what we* "*per-*

" *perceive*, that makes ſo much uſeleſs noiſe " and diſpute in the world:" he ſeems to give his ſanction to the moſt ſimple and ſatisfactory deſcription of *knowledge*, that can be comprehended in a few words.

In the next chapter, Mr. Locke treats of the degrees of knowledge: of theſe he enumerates the *intuitive*, the *demonſtrative*, and towards the end, with ſome heſitation, as if conſcious of inconſiſtency, he mentions the *ſenſitive* knowledge of particular exiſtence *. The intuitive he makes to conſiſt in the immediate perception of the agreement or diſagreement between two ideas,

* It is evident, that if we perceive only ideas, we can have no perception of particular exiſtence. Mr. Locke's embarraſſment proceeds from one or both of theſe cauſes: 1. He ſeems deſirous to explain the mechaniſm of thinking; and 2. To give ſuch an explanation, as ſhall comprehend both memory and perception; hence he talks only of the perception and compariſon of *ideas*.

ideas, without the intervention of any other. " Demonſtrative knowledge," he goes on to obſerve, " is where the mind " perceives the agreement, or diſagreement, " of any ideas, but not immediately." " The reaſon," he ſoon afterwards adds, " why the mind cannot always perceive " preſently," (i. e. at once) " the agree- " ment or diſagreement of two ideas is, " becauſe thoſe ideas, concerning whoſe " agreement or diſagreement the enquiry " is made, cannot by the mind be ſo put " together as to ſhew it *. In this caſe " then, when the mind cannot ſo bring

* Would it not be more ſimple to ſay, that we cannot contrive any ſingle experiment, which ſhall exhibit the reſult in queſtion? Thus we cannot ſhew at once, the equality of the angles of a triangle to two right angles. Whether the mind can or cannot bring the ideas together, depends entirely on the power of the eye.

" its

"its ideas together, as by their immediate "comparifon, and as it were, juxtapofition, "or application to one another, to per- "ceive their agreement or difagreement, "it is fain, by the intervention of other "ideas ... to difcover the agreement or "difagreement, which it fearches; and this "is what we call reafoning. Thus the mind "being willing to know the agreement "or difagreement in bignefs, between the "three angles of a triangle and two right "ones, cannot by an immediate view and "comparing them, do it: *becaufe the three* "*angles of a triangle cannot be brought at* "*once, and be compared with any one or two* "*angles*; and fo of this the mind has no "immediate, no intuitive knowledge. In "this cafe the mind is fain to find out fome "other angles, to which the three angles "of a triangle have an equality; and find- "ing thofe equal to two right ones, comes "to know their equality to two right ones.

"Thoſe intervening ideas, which ſerve to "ſhew the agreement of any two others "are called *proofs*, and where the agree-"ment or diſagreement is by this means "plainly and clearly perceived, it is called "*Demonſtration*." (B. IV. ch. ii. §. 2.)

In §. 7, he gives this deſcription of the proceſs of demonſtrative reaſoning. "*In* "*every ſtep* reaſon makes in demonſtrative "knowledge, there is an intuitive know-"ledge of that agreement or diſagreement "it ſeeks with the next intermediate idea "which it uſes, as a proof. For if it were "not ſo, that yet would need a proof; "ſince without the perception of ſuch "agreement or diſagreement there is no "knowledge produced; if it be perceived "by itſelf, it is intuitive knowledge: if it "cannot be perceived by itſelf, there is "need of ſome intervening idea, as a "common meaſure to ſhew their agree-"ment or diſagreement. By which it is

"plain

"plain, that every ſtep in reaſoning that "produces knowledge, has intuitive cer- "tainty."

There is only a ſlight difference in terms between this theory and that which I have endeavoured to explain, and to confirm by examples. And this difference of terms is owing to the independant origin of the latter. It vaniſhes altogether, as ſoon as it is obſerved, that intuitive and experimental knowledge are one and the ſame thing. The reader, I ſuppoſe, will not in this caſe think it neceſſary to attend to the common diſtinction between *obſervation* and *experiment*; to our perceptions it is of no conſequence, whether we diſpoſe objects on purpoſe to obſerve them, or are mere ſpectators. The perception is the ſame by whatever agency the objects are preſented to the ſenſes; though in geometry, we meet with infinitely more reſults of *experi-*

ment than of *observation* *, for we go on perpetually making experiments and accumulating results.

Clear as it is, no use has, I believe, yet been made of Mr. Locke's account of demonstrative evidence, either to solve difficulties or to improve the method of teaching in geometry: the shame, however, will be divided between so many culprits, and some of them so illustrious, that the share of each will be exceedingly small. For the subject has not fallen into the hands of ordinary compilers merely. Among the commentators upon Euclid, one might enumerate men of comprehensive views and various

* We have these results of *observation* in other passages of Euclid, besides the *axioms* of the first book. The first, second, and other propositions of the fifth book are *self-evident*, that is, we assent to them as soon as we understand the terms, which could not be, if we were not acquainted with appearances, warranting the result.

infor-

information; and authors, who aſpire far beyond the commentator's higheſt praiſe, have formally diſcuſſed the nature of mathematical evidence.

The great celebrity of a modern ſyſtem of pneumatology, conſpires with the opportunity I have had of conſulting it, ſince the beginning of this eſſay was ſent to the preſs, to induce me to alter the reſoſolution I originally formed, to avoid the quotation and diſcuſſion of different opinions. The author of this ſyſtem is Mr. Kant, Profeſſor at Koenigſberg in Pruſſia. Mr. Kant has raiſed to himſelf throughout Germany, a reputation ſuperior to that of Wolf, and at leaſt equal to that of Leibnitz. Among his numerous followers he reckons men of eminence, who having firſt violently oppoſed his doctrines have, by a tranſition not uncommon, become his zealous advocates: nor does that oppoſition which

which new opinions always have to encounter, ſeem to have ſerved any other purpoſe than to diffuſe thoſe of Mr. Kant. They have already been publicly taught at Jena, and there is reaſon to believe that they are making their way at Gottingen *. At a period when full liberty of ſentiment is happily eſtabliſhed throughout the republic of letters, ſpeculations which have ſo powerfully influenced independant minds, are an object of rational curioſity; and an inquiſitive perſon might wiſh, that an explicit account of Mr. Kaut's doctrines were publiſhed in Engliſh, which the terminology would render a difficult undertaking.

Mr. Kant, as might be expected in "*a critical examination of reaſon*," treats at

* See Gotting. Anzeig. p. 201. where in giving an account of Mr. Schultz's commentary upon Mr. Kant's moſt celebrated work, one of the Gottingen profeſſors half avows his converſion to the new ſyſtem.

large

large of the nature of demonſtration. The following quotation may ſerve in ſome meaſure to ſhew, in what light he conſiders it. I do not expect that it will do him much credit in this country, but it is unfair to judge an author ſo celebrated from a ſingle paſſage; a great work may doubtleſs contain much truth blended with a good deal of error. For my own part, I think that after Mr. Locke's diſcoveries, and thoſe relating to language, what chiefly remains to be done is, to digeſt the whole into an uniform ſyſtem, and to apply this ſyſtem to improve, or more properly ſpeaking, to create *the art of inſtruction.*

Mr. Kant aſſerts, "that we are in poſ-"ſeſſion of knowledge *a priori* *." In proof of his poſition he obſerves, "that in "order to make this appear, we have but

* Kritik der reinen Vernunſt, 1787. p. 3.

"to

" to discover a criterion by which to dis-" tinguish between *pure* and *empirical* know-" ledge. Now experience teaches us, that " a thing is so, but by no means that it " cannot be otherwise. If therefore there " be, 1. A proposition, which, when con-" ceived, is accompanied with an idea of " its necessity; this is a judgment *a priori.* " Any proposition too, deduced from ano-" ther, which is itself a necessary propo-" sition, is altogether *a priori.* 2. Expe-" rience never gives to its positions a real " and strict, but only an assumed and com-" parative universality; i. e. one derived " from induction. So that in propriety " we should say, that *as far as we have* " *hitherto observed, this or that rule admits* " *of no exception.* If therefore a proposi-" tion be conceived as strictly universal, or " in such a manner, that no exception is " allowed possible, this is not derived from

" expe-

" experience, but comes *a priori.* Empi-" rical universality is therefore only an ar-" bitrary extension of that which holds in " most cases to all cases, without excepti-" on; as in this proposition, *all bodies are* " *heavy.* On the contrary, where strict " universality essentially appertains to any " judgment, this circumstance points out " a peculiar origin of such judgments, viz. " a power of knowledge (*ein vermoegen des* " *erkenntnisses*) *a priori.* Necessity there-" fore and strict universality are sure crite-" rions of knowledge *a priori*; and they are " inseparably connected. But as in the ap-" plication of these criterions it is some-" times easier to point out the empirical " limitation of knowledge, than contin-" gency in our judgments, and again, as " the unlimited universality we attribute " to any judgment (or proposition,) is often " more obvious than its necessity, it is, for " these reasons, adviseable to use separately

" these

" these two criterions, of which each is " by itself infallible.

" That ſuch neceſſary and univerſal, and " conſequently pure judgments *a priori*, " may be found in human knowledge, it " is eaſy to ſhew. If you chooſe an ex- " ample from ſcience, I refer you *to all the* " *propoſitions in mathematics*: if you would " have one from the moſt common exer- " ciſe of the underſtanding, the propoſi- " tion, that *every change muſt have a cauſe*, " may ſerve for this purpoſe. Indeed the " idea of a cauſe, ſo obviouſly contains the " idea of the neceſſity of connection with " an effect, and a ſtrict univerſality of the " rule, that it (the idea of a cauſe) would " be entirely loſt, if with Hume we were " to deduce it from the frequent aſſocia- " tion of ſomething that happens with " ſomething that precedes, and from an " habit thence acquired of connecting the " ideas,

" ideas, confequently were to reduce it to " a fubjective neceffity, or a neceffity re- " lative to the obferver *."

This paffage, as I apprehend it, includes a confiderable number of miftakes; fome more, fome lefs, immediately connected with

* Modern writers, in our own language, exprefs an opinion, fimilar to that of Mr. Kant, and inevitably fatal to their philofophy of mind. " In flating the " argument for the exiftence of the Deity, fays Mr. " Stuart, feveral modern philofophers (as Dr. Reid) " have been at pains to illuftrate that law of our na- " ture, which leads us to refer every change we per- " ceive in the univerfe, to the operation of an effi- " cient caufe;" (or as he juft before terms it a *meta-phyfical* caufe, i. e. " fomething which is fuppofed to " be neceffarily connected with the change, and with- " out which it could not have happened.") " This " reference, he continues, is not the refult of reafon- " ing, but neceffarily accompanies the perception; " fo as to render it impoffible for us to fee the change, " without feeling a conviction of the operation of " fome

with the ſubject of mathematical reaſoning. At the riſque of a little apparent digreſſion, I ſhall endeavour to point out the principal of theſe miſtakes. To conſider Mr. Kant's ſecond example firſt;—*cauſe*, from being the name of a particular object, has become, in conſequence of the obliteration

" ſome cauſe, by which it was produced; much in " the ſame manner in which we find it impoſſible " to conceive a ſenſation, without being impreſſed " with the belief of the exiſtence of a ſentient being." *Philoſophy of the H. Mind*, 1792, p. 73. Dr. Reid, I think, always miſtakes our *habits* of obſervation for *original laws* of thought, and ſeems not ſufficiently acquainted with the nature of complex terms. In the inſtance here quoted, the term *ſenſation* comprehends *ſentient* beings, as *pride* does proud beings, and *yawning* yawning beings; or, as *two* includes *one* and *one*. When we therefore conceive the meaning of theſe terms, we find that like all others, they include their own ſignification, or ſignify what they do ſignify, which, I ſuppoſe, is all the remark amounts to.

of

of that original ſignification, a remarkable abbreviation in language. If a perſon aſks himſelf, what is a cauſe? he will find that he has no idea affixed to the term; and can only explain it by the ſubſtitution of a particular object taken from a particular fact, or by ſaying that it means "ſomething which precedes ſomething elſe." Thus when electricity is ſaid to be *the cauſe* of thunder and lightning, we mean that thunder and lightning will never be obſerved, unleſs the electrical fluid be firſt unequally diſtributed. As ſoon as we trace back the word to its original meaning, (when only we can be ſaid to have an idea of it) we ſhall find that it includes no idea of neceſſity; and in this manner the etymologiſt will generally correct the errors of the metaphyſician. Thus, cauſſa *ſeu* cauſa, ſays Mr. Scheid, a *καυσω futuro thematis καυω propriè* pungo, ſtimulo, *unde* κᾶυσις, cauſa, *ut a* πᾶυσις, pauſa. Cautes c. q. καυϛης, *unde* cauterium, *a* κεκαυϛαι, *ib.* καυω, pungo (*Etymol. p.* 1183). Lennep. (ibid. p. 380.) obſerves, that in καιω, the ſame word with καυω, only differently ſpelled, the ſignification of burning is ſecondary to that of pricking. Thus, καιω, uro: Ortum eſt *a ſimpliciori* καω, *cujus notio propria quærenda eſt in* motu rei impulſæ & ſtimulatæ. Thus we ſee the term *cauſe* originating in the motion produced in living animals, by the application of a pointed body occaſioning pain. People in general are as little conſcious of *cauſe* having any proper ſignification, as of one of the letters of the alphabet having a proper ſignification; and could language have been formed after the knowledge of its principles, we might as well have taken one of the letters of the alphabet for ſuch an abbreviation. And then I ſuppoſe we ſhould never

never have heard of an idea of cauſe, independent of obſervation and experience. It is curious to remark, how we uſe *cauſe* in a ſenſe not only remote from its proper ſenſe, but often at croſs purpoſes with it: thus we may either ſay, *corpulency is the cauſe of indolence*, or, *indolence is the cauſe of corpulency*. Inſtead of cauſe, it would ſeem ſtrange if we were to read, *ſtimulus*, *ſpur*, or *goad*.

Cauſes or *events preceding other events*, may perhaps be arranged, with reſpect to our manner of obſerving them, in three claſſes. 1. Thoſe of which we are mere inactive, though attentive ſpectators; of ſuch cauſes aſtronomy, geology, medicine and phyſiology, ſupply abundant examples. 2. Thoſe of which we acquire the knowledge, by diſpoſing objects purpoſely to obſerve the ſucceſſion of events, as in certain phyſical inveſtigations. 3. Thoſe of which we acquire the knowledge by our moſt ſimple and earlieſt obſervations and experiments, as of impulſe producing motion. This laſt claſs differs from the preceding, only in date, and in being unaccompanied with the remembrance of meditation. But the ſpontaneous and early origin of the knowledge of theſe laſt cauſes, has deceived the philoſophers. They have taken away from experience the credit of our inſtruction, for want of perceiving how early ſhe begins her leſſons.

Neceſſity, like *cauſe*, is a mere abbreviation, and we have no idea of neceſſity more than of cauſe: neceſſity is ſo looſe a term, that by obſerving various phraſes, in which it occurs, we ſhall perceive that it ſtands as a ſubſtitute for the moſt diſſimilar ideas. When a maſter ſays to his ſervant, "it is neceſſary that you be more ſober henceforward," he means, "unleſs you be more ſober,

ſober, I ſhall diſcharge you :" or a phyſician to his patient; " it is neceſſary you take this medicine ;"—he means, " if you do not take this medicine, be aſſured you will not recover ;" that is to ſay, when reſolved farther into experience, " he has " ſeen, or others have ſeen, the medicine " cure the diſorder." Thus it is, that the forms of ſpeaking have uniformly deceived metaphyſicians; and thus all words, and combinations of words, may be referred to perceptions of ſenſe, and none can mean any thing beyond obſervation.

To obſervation and to induction alone, whatever Mr. Kant may imagine, it is eaſy to ſee that we owe our knowledge of the abſolute neceſſity or ſtrict univerſality of geometrical truths: one cannot indeed be ſurprized, that the induction of particulars ſhould have eſcaped thoſe whom the nature of the reaſoning has totally eſcaped. Every one of us, by calling to mind the train of his own thoughts, may aſſure himſelf that, in ſtudying Euclid, however rapid, and however eaſy the proceſs of induction, we have at leaſt, in imagination, varied the forms of the diagrams, and finding the reaſoning equally applicable to all imaginable varieties, have aſſented to the truth of the propoſitions. A beginner, eſpecially if he be young, will not be ſatisfied even in the ſimpleſt caſe, till he has gone through the proceſs of induction. He will actually ſtop to vary the interſections and approximations of two ſtraight lines, till he is convinced by experiment, that they cannot incloſe ſpace; at leaſt, he will ſtop to imagine theſe ſimple experiments. One inſtance I have myſelf ſeen, and I ſuppoſe they are not uncommon, of a ſtudent drawing a figure anew upon a different ſcale, in order to ſatisfy himſelf, that the demonſtration

ſtration was not confined to the particular figure before him: and teachers, I believe, at ſetting out, ſeldom fail to call the attention of their hearers to this induction. "You ſee," they remark, "that the rea-"ſoning does not concern this or that par-"ticular ſhape or ſize of triangles, &c." A little conſideration ſatisfies the pupil, that the induction is full and perfect; and hence the ſtrict univerſality of mathematical truths.

The propoſition, quoted by Mr. Kant, *that all bodies are heavy*, does not ſupply a fair object of compariſon with geometrical propoſitions. Plane triangles, parallel lines, and the various kinds of ſolids, are definite things; clear perceptions fix the meaning of the term. But this is not the caſe with *all poſſible bodies*.

Mr. Locke has already obſerved, that intuitive is clearer and more certain than demonſtrative knowledge; and this, in as far as they differ, is unqueſtionably true; that which is immediately before the ſenſes, impreſſes us always with the moſt lively conviction. The ſphere of viſion when diſtinct is very limited; we are obliged to view things in ſucceſſion; and I ſuppoſe that the memory cannot bring more knowledge before the mind at once, than the eye can at once receive; moſt certainly no memory can offer at once that chain of experiments, by which it is ſhewn, that the ſquare of the hypothenuſe is equal to the ſquares of the two other ſides of a right-angled triangle. Every one muſt be conſcious, that if this truth could be exhibited to the eye at once, could it by any mechanical contrivance be made the firſt propoſition in geometry; our conviction would be more lively than that which we obtain from a number of reſults. What we ſee will ever ſeem more certain than what we remember to have ſeen; and when we have drawn out a long chain of conſequences, ſome latent apprehenſion will remain, that we may not have examined each ſucceſſive link, in a ſtate of perfect freedom from illuſion of ſenſe and diſtraction of thought. It is not then with much propriety that the anatomiſts have been reprehended for profaning a term, which ſome metaphyſicians would conſecrate and ſet apart to mathematical certainty. What is *ſhewn* to us by anatomy, we are juſt as ſure of, as of that which is *ſhewn* to us by geometry.

Mr. Locke felt that demonſtration is not limited to quantity. "It has been generally," ſays he, "taken for granted, that "mathematics alone are capable of demonſtrative certainty. But to have ſuch an "agreement or diſagreement, as may in- "tuitively

" tuitively be perceived, being, as I imagine, not the privilege of the ideas of " *number*, *extenſion* and *figure* alone, it may " poſſibly be the want of due method and " application in us, and not of ſufficient " evidence in things, that demonſtration " has been thought to have ſo little to do " in other parts of knowledge, and been " ſcarce ſo much as aimed at by any but " mathematicians. For whatever ideas we " have, wherein the mind can perceive the " immediate agreement or diſagreement " there is between them, there the mind " is capable of intuitive knowledge; and " where it can perceive the agreement or " diſagreement of any two ideas, by an " intuitive perception of the agreement or " diſagreement they have with any intermediate ideas, there the mind is capable " of demonſtration, which is not limited

" to

" to ideas of extenſion, number, figure, " and their modes." (IV. 6. §. 9.)

Wherever we have clear perceptions, there doubtleſs we have the full evidence of demonſtration. It is as certain to me, that ſugar is ſoluble in water, as that two ſtraight lines can never encloſe a ſpace; or in Mr. Locke's more complicated language, my mind perceives as perfectly the agreement of the ideas of ſugar, and of ſolution in water, as it does the diſagreement of the ideas of two ſtraight lines, and incloſed ſpace. I may not ſo readily recognize ſugar and water, as I do certain figures of plane geometry, nor with ſuch certainty as I do all the plane figures and ſolids of geometry without exception. Now on this *facility* and *certainty* of recognition muſt depend the facility and certainty of the application of our knowledge. And as we can apply knowledge more readily, the

more

more perfectly do we seem to possess it; in whatever light therefore we view it, we discover the absolute dependance of mathematical knowledge upon sense. And what our senses are so perfectly adequate to convey, they have been supposed not to convey at all; just as we many times hardly perceive ourselves doing, what we do with perfect ease. In comparing physical with mathematical knowledge, we shall find certainty arising, in the latter case, from the perfect competency of our senses, in the former from their incompetency. What for instance is it, that prevents me from being as certain, that water consists of hydrogene and oxygene airs, as of any proposition in Euclid?—nothing surely but the incompetency of my senses. In the first place, I cannot perceive whether these airs do not previously contain a large quantity of water: secondly, the heat that appears,

pears, and of which I have no adequate perception, perplexes me; and thirdly, the occasional appearance of an acid in the water. Now if I could perceive the small quantity of azotic air present, separately uniting with a certain portion of the oxygene air to form acid, while the hydrogene air unites with the rest to form water; if I could see that the airs previously contain only a little or no water beforehand, and if there was no heat and light, I should have demonstrative evidence—and that just as clear as that mucilage of gum arabic consists of water and of that particular gum, or that suds consist of soap and water.

Thus when the senses serve us imperfectly, and make us continually feel our dependance, we are ever ready to acknowledge the obligation. But where they instantly deliver such clear and full perceptions

tions to the memory, that we have no more occaſion to recur to them, we forget or deny the ſervice they have rendered us. —It is ſaid, that the ſtateſman, after the final ſucceſs of his intrigues, is apt to ſpurn away the ladder by which he has mounted to power. In like manner the metaphyſician, when he feels his mind elevated to what he calls *abſtraction*, or when his thoughts are employed about objects, of which the remembrance is almoſt as diſtinct as the perception, is apt to betray an inattention equal to the ſtateſman's ingratitude.

Pure phyſical ſcience ſeems faſt approaching to the fullneſs and clearneſs of mathematical ſcience; an obſervation of which more examples will be found in Mr. Lavoiſier's Elementary Treatiſe of Chemiſtry, than in any other book I am acquainted with. By contrivances calculated to convey the moſt diſtinct perceptions, he every where

where impreſſes a degree of conviction, which, not many years ago, would have been thought unattainable in the ſtudy of impalpable ſubſtances *. The different kinds of air may perhaps be conſidered, with reſpect to our ſenſes, as occupying a middle place between palpable bodies and the *ætherial* fluids, if any ſuch exiſt. Perhaps

* Mr. Condorcet, who poſſeſſes vaſt extent as well as accuracy of knowledge, and whoſe mathematical ſkill is well known, has lately expreſſed himſelf in the following manner concerning mathematical, compared with other, truths.—Mr. Buffon etablit cette opinion, que les verités mathematiques ne ſont point des verités reelles, mais de pures verités de definition; obſervaſion juſte, ſi on veut la prendre dans la rigueur metaphyſique, mais qui *s'applique egalement alors aux verités de tous les ordres*, deſqu'elles ſont preciſes & qu'elles n'ont pas des individus pour objet. Si enſuite, on veut appliquer ces verités a la pratique et les rendre dés—lors individuelles, *ſemblables encore en cet egard* a des verités mathematiques, elles ne ſont plus que des verités

haps another Lavoiſier, by bringing theſe as much within the ſphere of the ſenſes, may exhibit almoſt mathematical evidence of the qualities of *fire*, *electricity* and *magnetiſm.*

To ſolid geometry we do not come any thing near ſo well prepared by obſervation as to plane. The difficulty of *imagining* (which

verités approchées. Il n'exiſte reellement qu'une ſeule difference, c'eſt que les idées, dont l'identité forme les verités mathematiques & phyſiques ſont plus abſtraites dans les premiéres, d' ou il reſulte que pour les verités phyſiques, nous avons un, ſouvenir diſtinct des individus, dont elles expriment les qualités communes; & que nous ne l'avons pour les autres: mais la veritable realité, l' utilité d'une propoſition quelconque eſt independante de cette difference; car on doit regarder une verité comme reelle toutes les fois que, ſi on l'applique a un objet reellement exiſtant, elle reſte un verité abſolue, ou devient une verité indefiniment approchée.—*Hiſtoire de l'Acad. des Sciences, pour l'année*, 1788. p. 64. *Paris*, 1791.

In

(which always depends on the want of opportunity, or of power to *perceive*) the intersections of solids, is always very sensibly felt. And here it is almost as necessary as in mechanics, to exhibit the objects, whose qualities are to be taught; and to call in the joint assistance of the hands and eyes. So far, if experiment mean the disposal of

In stating the only difference which he believes to subsist between mathematical and other truths, Mr. Condorcet is not, in my opinion, perfectly accurate. The individual objects, of which we retain the remembrance, must excite a number of perceptions; and all or several of these, joined together, form the character. Now objects, presenting but one or two circumstances to notice, can scarce have an individual character; we think no more of the individual glass of water upon which we have made any observation, than upon the individual triangle or square. So also in a great number of physical truths besides, we have *not* any distinct recollection of the individuals, whose common properties these truths express.

objects for the purpose of observing them, most teachers, doubtless, find it not less necessary to make experiments formally in the science of quantity than in that of motion.

Mathematics, in fine, teach either to measure or to count. The simplest and the shortest way we can acquire either of these arts, the better, I believe, in all respects. We cannot possibly set about to learn either of them otherwise *, than by the use of the senses. And it is by no means impossible,

* Children may be observed to learn to count with great labour, and it is long before they learn the terms of number perfectly.—If you lay a very small number of similar objects before a child, that has been learning to count for some time, and ask how many there are, he will be obliged to stretch out his hand, tell them over slowly. The eye, which takes its other lessons so admirably from the touch, never attains much readiness in the discrimination of number. No person, I apprehend, can distinguish eleven from twelve similar objects at a glance.

ſible, that there may be a method of applying the ſenſes, in geometry at leaſt, to far greater advantage than any practiſed at preſent; a method at once agreeable, expeditious, and calculated to invigorate every mental faculty. When ſuch a plan of education ſhall be generally adopted, (and its outline is not extremely difficult to trace) that more knowledge than the learned and ſcientific now uſually poſſeſs at forty, may be acquired by twenty, ſuch a method of teaching geometry will probably form part of it.

If *all we know* be, as it aſſuredly is, juſtly reduced by Mr. Locke to intuition, (or perception, for demonſtration is but a ſucceſſion of intuitions or perceptions), *all we believe or expect* muſt be founded upon what others have reported concerning their intuitions, in addition to our own. And all evidence may therefore, I think, moſt conveniently be referred to two general heads; either, 1. What we ourselves have personally experienced, or *direct evidence:* or, 2. What other persons assert, that they have experienced, or *indirect evidence.* Thus we are confined within the circle of sense by a spell cast upon every individual of the human race, and such as we can never by any efforts dissolve.

Under the two heads of direct and indirect evidence, there are an infinite number of gradations of credibility; in our opinion concerning almost each particular, whether falling under the cognizance of our senses or testified by others, we may acquiesce with a different degree of conviction. Should any one ask, But how, since our senses are fallible, shall we then attain to certainty? It can only be replied, that certainty is not among the privileges of our nature, except *that certainty*

tainty which is attainable by ſenſe. Infallibility was never, as far as I know, guaranteed to man; nor is there any danger leſt, like the Children in the Wood, we ſhould lay us down and die, leſt we ſhould fall into the pit of error. We differ from one another in every circumſtance of conduct, taſte, and ſentiment with perfect ſelf-ſatisfaction; and opinions for which he has only weak indirect evidence, each man entertains with the fulleſt aſſurance, notwithſtanding he has againſt him the bulk of his ſpecies. Often as human proneneſs to error is bewailed, it does not appear that many among us feel a ſincere anxiety for that degree of certainty, any more than for that extent of knowledge, of which we are perfectly capable.

Opinions were unfortunately, long prevalent in the world, of which the direct tendency was to deprive men of the moſt valuable, as being the moſt certain, portion of knowledge; namely, that which we acquire from our intuitions. Now there is, I am diſpoſed to believe, no abſurdity of opinion which is not productive of ſome pernicious practice. Even when the opinions are renounced and forgotten, the practices, into which they have deluded mankind, may ſtill prevail for ages. Of this truth, I either fancy or find a deplorable proof in the common conduct of liberal education. And if Mr. Locke * has in vain diſcovered the principles upon which education ought to proceed, and in vain applied them with great, but not unexceptionable ſkill, I attribute his want of ſucceſs, very much to

* I by no means forget Mr. Locke's great predeceſſor, Bacon, of whoſe *Advancement of Learning* I wiſh to ſee a new 8vo. edition. The common old thin 4to. is not adapted to modern delicacy in books, and it is not indeed a pleaſant book to read.

the

the deep impreſſion left by the *Antient Metaphyſics*. We know how ſtudiouſly Plato depreciated the body, the ſenſes, and the informations of ſenſe; how his excommunication of our perceptive powers was confirmed by the peripatetic *phantaſms*, and how both were amalgamated with the fantaſtic religious opinions, that ſo long bewildered and brutalized mankind; as alſo what authority this monſtrous mixture of heterogeneous reveries maintained during a long ſucceſſion of ages. "The Platoniſts," ſays Mr. Harris *, "conſidering ſcience as "ſomething aſcertained, definite and ſteady "would admit nothing to be its object "which was vague, indefinite and paſſing. "For this reaſon they excluded all indivi-"duals or objects of ſenſe, and, as Am-"monius expreſſes it, raiſed themſelves in

* Treatiſes, p. 341.

" their contemplations from beings parti- " cular to beings univerſal, and which " from their own nature, were eternal " and durable——.

" Conſonant to this, was the advice of " Plato, with reſpect to the progreſs of " our ſpeculations and inquiries, to deſcend " from thoſe higher genera, which include " many ſubordinate ſpecies, down to the " loweſt rank of ſpecies, thoſe which in- " clude only individuals. But here it was " his opinion that our enquiries ſhould " ſtop, AND AS TO INDIVIDUALS LET " THEM WHOLLY ALONE; becauſe of " theſe there could not poſſibly be any " ſcience."

Such were the ravings of the parent of myſticiſm. And as the Barbarians of the Weſt could not but ſurvey with an enthuſiaſm, bordering on adoration, the fine compoſitions of the antient writers, this ſenti-

ſentiment greatly contributed, by an obvious aſſociation, to their baneful effect.

What has been the progreſs of phyſical and moral ſcience, ſince their cultivators have gone directly contrary to the *advice* of Plato, is well underſtood. The ſcience of grammar has been juſt created upon preciſely the ſame principle; but moral, phyſical, and grammatical inſtruction, which, as well as diſcovery, muſt in order to be efficacious, proceed from the obſervation, or, if you pleaſe, the exhibition of particulars, is ſtill conducted after Plato's own heart; and were he now to viſit our ſeminaries, there is every reaſon to preſume, that this contemplator of *beings univerſal*, would be ſatisfied with our conformity to his injunctions. For aſſuredly, we neglect, as much as in us lies, the cultivation of all ſuch knowledge as the ſenſes convey, and we let individuals wholly alone.

alone. The conſequence is, that when the term of education has elapſed, the greater number find themſelves utterly deſtitute and helpleſs; without an outline which they can afterwards agreeably employ themſelves in filling up, and with few or no acquiſitions which they can apply to the ſervice of others. The few, who feel the pride of ſuperior powers, have nothing upon which to pique themſelves, but certain pretenſions to *taſte*.

Theſe pretenſions, I believe, ſhew, on the one hand, how, according to Mr. Locke, men, after eſpouſing certain well-endowed or faſhionable opinions, "ſeek arguments, either to make good their beauty, or varniſh over and cover their deformity;" while, on the other, they furniſh an inſtance, where more than ordinary penetration is required to make a diſcovery, or more than ordinary ingenuouſneſs

ousness to produce a confession; one may expect indeed, that a man will keep such a secret as long as he can from himself as well as from others; for however much he may have laboured, and however regularly he may have passed through the forms, he must either summon up resolution to begin anew, or perpetually carry about with him a most humiliating consciousness.

Where the taste has been almost exclusively cultivated, the character will be without energy, and its most prominent feature will be that *delicacy of feeling*, against which Mr. Hume has entered so just a protest. Gray, stripped of his genius, is a tolerably fair model of a man of mere taste; and nothing can be well imagined less desireable, than Gray's sickly constitution of mind. Nothing, I think, affords a more lively representation of intellects thus puny and pas-

sive

ſive than thoſe maſſes of animated jelly, which one ſees at times ſcattered along the ſea ſhore, without bone or tendon, that quiver to every blaſt and ſhrink at every touch.

The futility of this plea in defence of a method, according to which more time is conſumed and more drudgery undergone, than would be ſufficient to learn half the Encyclopedia in addition to all that is really acquired, plainly appears from the aſſociation of the moſt exquiſite taſte with the greateſt proficiency in phyſical knowledge. Such an aſſociation has frequently been ſeen in our times; in Haller, Born, Buffon, Murray, Darwin, and twenty others *. It will more and more frequently be

* Mr. Heyne, whoſe taſte and judgment will not be diſputed, ſpeaks always in as high terms of *real* or phyſical knowledge, as Bacon himſelf.—— " Naturæ vero cognoſcendæ ſtudium, omnis veræ philoſophiæ

be ſeen, as we diſcard more and more of the inveterate errors and inadequate inſtitutions of our anceſtors. It is impoſſible to doubt that out of every hundred of liberally educated perſons, whatever be the extent of their capacity, ninety *might* have acquired as correct a taſte and infinitely more knowledge than they poſſeſs.

As claſſical literature is not the whole, nor the moſt important part of that which ought to be taught in the courſe of a good education, ſo even to acquire this, ſome better method than that which we at preſent follow is wanting *. In fact, many of thoſe,

phiæ fundus, humanæ mentis fax certiſſima—*ad ea quoque, quæ extra ſenſibilem naturam poſita eſſe dicuntur.*" Opuſc. iii. 204.

* Hemſterhuſius, ſays Mr. Ruhnken, *commentitias anomalias, quibus grammatici omnia perturbaſſent, ex, loſit, denique tenebras linguæ (Græcæ nempe) per tot ſæcula of-fuſas*

those, who are made to devote years to the pursuit, approach no nearer to the object, than

fusas ita discussit, ut qua linguâ nulla est neque verbis neque formis copiosior, eâdem JAM *nulla reperiatur ad discendum facilior.*

Our school boys, I am much afraid, know nothing of the consummation announced by Mr. Ruhnken's JAM, however devoutly they may wish for it. They feel what Lennep says will be the case, as long as the Greek language is taught according to our barbarous grammars—*nihil tristius ejus studiis invenietur; nihil quod possit juventutem ab ejus linguæ culturâ, deterrere magis.* We are unacquainted with those few and simple rules, *ad quas omnia in linguis, tanquam ad normam certissimam, exigi possint; quas ex ipsâ linguæ naturâ ductas, & ratione suffultas, memoriæ infigere, & infixas conservare diutissime possis* (p. 4.).

Assuredly, if the spirit of the classics be so salutary to the youthful mind, we should infuse it as effectually as possible. Now, besides those quoted above, there is other high authority for supposing, that our methods are not so effectual as those practised elsewhere.

I ——Some

than children when they give chace to the extremity of the rainbow. Nor is any thing more

——Some years ago, the king, ſuppoſing that our ſchool editions of the claſſics, might be uſeful in his German Dominions, ordered a collection of the books uſed at Weſtminſter and Eton to be ſent to Mr. Heyne, at Gottingen. Of theſe editions Mr. H. has publiſhed a review, (Gottingen Magazine, 1780, No. 6, p. 429, &c.): he marks the greater number with a ſtrong note of diſapprobation. He is ſtruck by the metrical part of our Latin grammar; obſerves, that it muſt needs be very crabbed and obſcure; and ſeems to doubt, whether we are quite ſo abſurd as to force children to learn it by rote. It is, indeed, to be hoped, that this moſt painful inſtrument of grammatical torture will ſoon be generally laid aſide. Our claſſical ſcholars would perhaps wiſh, that the whole of this Review might be tranſlated; and were Mr. H.'s remonſtrances likely to produce an alteration, it would be a work of humanity to tranſlate it: but I ſuſpect that the immediate effect would be to alarm our pride, rather than correct our errors, as the following expreſſions, more common than to see the school and college books, finally consigned over to the damps and cobwebs of the dark closet, the moment their possessor becomes *sui juris.*

pressions, which may be considered as a summary of this celebrated professor's opinion on our method of instruction in the Latin, may serve to shew: "Experience, he says, proves, that good Latin is no "where more uncommon than among the English. "Their best scholars (*Humanisten*) often write a Latin "style, full of solecisms and barbarisms. Even in "some school-books the preface and additional matter are expressed in very bad Latin. At this no one "will be surprized, when he sees how they are introduced early in life, to the knowledge of Latin."

Mr. Heyne speaks in the most contemptuous terms of that, which Mr. Harris calls Dr. Clarke's "*rational edition of Homer*." The translation, he says, is barbarous, and a disgrace to the poet—the grammatical observations either false or trivial, the thousand times repeated references to which he thinks intolerable: the notes, he besides observes, seldom afford the illustration wanted, &c. &c.

It

It was partly in order to ſtrengthen, if poſſible, thoſe arguments that have been urged in favour of a plan of education which ſhall pay ſome attention to the ſenſes and the underſtanding, by many illuſtrious writers from Locke to Condorcet *; partly to take away from the revivers of exploded abſurdities, that ſupport which they have been deſirous to gain, by forcing into an unnatural alliance with their cauſe, ſo reſpectable a ſcience as mathematics; and partly to ſhew what falſe meaſures of objects are taken by thoſe who have no better rule than *antient metaphyſics*, that theſe remarks are offered to public conſideration. Had it not been for ſuch collateral views, that eminent patron of lite-

* In his memoirs on *public inſtruction*, in the *Bibliotheque de l'homme publique*.

rature, whoſe name may be read at the bottom of the title page, ſhould never have riſqued upon them the expence of paper and printing.

THE END.

NOTE I.

On the Syſtem of the Greek Language, propoſed by *Schultens*, *Hemſterhuis*, their Diſciples, and by Lord *Monboddo*.

Neque enim ad grammaticorum regulas linguæ fuerunt conditæ; ſed ex linguis multo uſu populorum jam tritis et excultis, regulæ tandem ſunt formatæ.

Lennep. de Analogiâ, p. 55.

IT ſeems to me hardly poſſible for a mere claſſical ſcholar to make any diſcovery of importance concerning the ſtructure of language. The little ſucceſs with which the long-continued efforts of ſuch ſcholars have been attended, and a conſideration of the Greek and Latin languages themſelves, concur in countenancing this opinion. The Greek language (and the Latin is ſcarcè any thing but a dialect of the Greek), has its ſurface ſo highly varniſhed, and its joints ſo cloſely fitted, that the acuteſt ſurveyor could hardly ever have aſcertained the original materials of which it is composed, or have distinguished the size and shape of the pieces that are thus nicely adapted to one another. Had not Schultens and Ten Kate deduced some just ideas from the study of languages, whose structure lies more open to inspection, I cannot easily persuade myself, that Hemsterhuis, or his disciples, Lennep and Valckenaer, would have contributed any thing material towards the philosophy of language. Their merit would, in all probability, have been confined to the purification of the Greek grammar from a few of its absurdities, and to the interpretation and amendment of passages in Greek authors.

That I may not be accused of lightly advancing this unfavourable surmise, I shall endeavour to render it probable, that their knowledge of Greek has served but to bewilder the Dutch Etymologists. The more, indeed, I consider their system of *analogy*, the more does it appear to me to be repugnant to every kind and degree of evidence, as well as productive of particular errors without end. Where one can judge of their positions with any sort of confidence, there they seem palpably erroneous; and in other cases, contrary to all probability. Nevertheless, what they have collected, when properly arranged, will be found

to

to confirm the true theory of language, by many very ſtriking facts.

I have already looſely obſerved, that their ſyſtem ſuppoſes a regular derivation of the language from a few ſhort primitives. Lord Monboddo, more conſiſtent and more ingenious, reduces without heſitation, the Greek primitives to the five duads already quoted, and had he turned his attention to the manner in which the vowels are formed by the organs of ſpeech, and perceived their near affinity, he might with juſt as much propriety have reduced all his primitives to one.

The Dutch etymologiſts do not all ſeem to have ſo much narrowed the baſe of their building. They aſſume triliteral and quadriliteral as well as biliteral roots, and are doubtful whether there are not quinqueliteral. *Inveſtigari poterit*, ſays Valckenaer, *quot probabiliter a* primis ſapientibus illis linguæ conditoribus, *ſimplicia primitiva fixa fuerint & conſtituta—Verba primitiva ab* Α *incipientia in antiquâ & ſimplici linguâ fuerunt tantum duodecim nempe,* ἄζω, ἄγω, ἄκω, ἄλω, ἄμω, ἄιω, ἄπω, ἄρω, ἄσω, ἄτω, et ἄω.——

Ab ακω, ακαω, ακεω, ακιω, ακοω, ακυω—and ſo on till you come by a regular increaſe, even to [illegible].— Again,

Ab αγω, αγκω, αγκαζω, αγαιω, αγαλλω, αγανω.—Mr. Scheid, when he calls the five biliteral, the moſt fimple roots, (Etym. p. xlvi and xlvii), feems to come nearer to Lord M. as does alfo Lennep, when he obferves, *manifeftum itaque eft, extitiffe in antiquâ linguâ Græcâ* has quinque *formas fimpliciffimas* (viz. the duads), *eafque adeo merito* primas *Græcæ linguæ* origines *dici.*

In this manner, then, by infertion of letters, and the confequent enlargement of words, was the whole language formed from a few roots. And, as Valckenaer further remarks, *ex verbis primitivis, tanquam totidem ftirpibus et radicibus, amano linguæ horto infitis, derivatorum verborum, tanquam totidem ramorum fœcunda propago emicuit et propullulavit.* And not only was the mode of the *derivation*, but that alfo of the *compofition*, of words fixed by thefe fame wife founders, who beheld in fpirit the future fortunes of their verbal progeny.—Verba *autem cum* verbis, & nomina *cum* nominibus *modo tam vario et tam artificiofo componi queunt, & fibi invicem innecti et illigari, ut componendi et glutinandi rationes, quas* PRIMI CONDITORES *linguæ admirabilis fixiffe videntur, nullis regulis includi poffe videantur,* (p. 22.)

How little probable, or rather how impoffible, any fuch formation of a language is, the hiftory of mankind evidently fhews. Upon what grounds can fuch a degree of forefight and tafte be imagined to have exifted isted among the Greeks before the historical times? and the inconceivable enterprize of laying out a language according to a regular plan, could not have escaped both history and tradition. The motives and the means of execution defy conception. If Aristotle and Plato could not see this artificial system, when the language lay actually before them, shall we believe that their remote and forgotten predecessors could call it up before their imagination? In truth, such a reach of thought is not the affair of untutored and uninspired mortals, who, as they had a language of art to form, must have spoken a rude language. Now in the condition of society, implied in this supposition, human life is divided between sensation, sleep, listlessness, and phrenzy; for the tumultuous sallies of the exalted imagination of a savage, fall nothing short of phrenzy. Such an effort of generalization one may therefore as reasonably expect from the remote ancestors of Homer, as an *Essay on Human Understanding* from an Hottentot.

If the other member of the dilemma be preferred, and these CONDITORES be placed in an age so cultivated as to have a written speech, the garden of language will, it is evident, be already occupied; nor will there be ſpace for theſe new roots, and the wide-ſpreading ſoliage of the trees which they produce *.

If we ſurvey a collection of Greek words analogically arranged †, and admit their affinity, we may form two ſuppoſitions; 1. That the long words are formed from the ſhort by extenſion; or, 2. The ſhort from the long by contraction. Now as we have no poſitive hiſtorical evidence to determine which of theſe

* *Conſideramus linguam Grecam, tanquam hortum ſimplici ac naturali pulchritudine amœniſſimum, gratâ florum diverſiſſimorum copiâ cultiſſimum, et mirificum in modum variegatum; ſed cujus horti præ ceteris hortis natura duplicem ob rationem eſt admirabilis;* primum, *quod ſi ſpectemus horti amplitudinem & capacitatem, arbores ferat numero pauciſſimas, arbores vero per eoſdem ordines directas; arbores, quorum proceritas & late ſpatioſa et in longum diffuſa ramorum amplitudo ſpatium horti totum opacet.* Deinde *id arboribus hujus horti peculiare eſt, quod truncus omnium arborum ſit ſimillimus, quod rami in omnibus arboribus numero pares ad eandem lineam videantur educti, quodque in ſingulis ramis omnium truncorum totidem reperiantur folia, nullis lineamentis diſparia, adeo ut qui unius rami folia, unius trunci ramos, oculo curioſo et philoſophico conſideraverit, ac probe perſpexerit, is eâdem operâ mox noverit, ſingularum arborum rami quot foliis gravati luxurientur, quot rami e ſingulis truncis propullulaverint.* (Valkenaer, p. 87.)

† Valckenaer, (p. 58, 69.) has an alphabetical arrangement of an hundred words derived from ἄω.

is the true fuppofition, fo neither in itfelf does the fyftem of analogical abbreviation appear more improbable than that of analogical elongation.

And the former fyftem is countenanced by all experience in languages. After they are written, and doubtlefs alfo before, they fhew a ftrong tendency to drop letters. If there be exceptions to this rule, they are afforded by a few words of infrequent ufe, or by words adopted from languages already in efteem, a caufe that never difturbed the natural tendency of the Greek language, or by fome very peculiar circumftance: as our adoption of *unlefs*, inftead of *lefs*, ufed by many of our old writers, was perhaps determined by our taking *lefs* for a term of comparifon. Here we neglect caufes which operate to fuch a fmall extent, as well as changes made merely *euphoniæ gratiâ*: Had the Greek language afforded this feries,

If, gif, yef, give, yeve, gin, given,

Mr. Valckenaer would doubtlefs have fixed upon *if* as the primitive. Yet wherever there is an opportunity of obferving fucceffive alterations in words, we fhall find abridgment and not extenfion; whether in the different periods of an improving language, or, (where it is exceedingly remarkable,) in the difference between the long concatenation of articulations in barbarous tongues, and

and the monoſyllables that form the baſe of written languages. We cannot but ſuppoſe, that this latter change has taken place by degrees; it is not very eaſy to believe, that words have the property of ſhutting up all at once, like pocket teleſcopes. Lord Monboddo, I know, pretends, that *languages of art* muſt be made by *men of art*, that is, by thoſe "who have made a "particular ſtudy of words and things, with a plan "or ſyſtem, proceeding in a certain method, and ac- "cording to certain rules for the attainment of that "end;" but, as uſual, he forgets to prove all this *. He

* Here is a ſpecimen of his Lordſhip's manner of arguing, &c. "It may be thought—that though there be, no doubt, a great deal "of art in language, yet it may have ariſen by degrees from "experience, obſervation, and vulgar uſe; and that in this way "even a language of art may have been formed without any re- "gular plan or ſyſtem. If this be true, I think it muſt be true "likewiſe, that all the other arts, liberal as well as mechanical, "muſt have been invented in the ſame way; *and that painting,* "*muſic, architecture, muſt have been the work of the* MERE VUL- "GAR!" II. 483. Some philoſophers have been as liberal in imputing *art*, or ingenious contrivance, to rude nations, as Lord M. (who quibbles not a little about the term *art*) is niggardly. Thus the *trial by jury* has been imputed to profound political wiſdom, as if a review had been taken of all *actual* and all *poſſible* modes

He informs us further, that "the inventors of the "art of language were men of authority among a sa-"vage people." (II. 497.) Now let us hear what task these savage men of authority had to perform: first, "A system of etymology was to be formed, by "which the whole language was to be derived from "certain primitive sounds, or radical words. Then "cases, genders and numbers were to be invented, "which answered a double purpose, both of expressing "different relations and other circumstances of things,

modes of administering justice; and this had been preferred upon comparison. But it is, in fact, a very obvious suggestion of our sense of justice, and follows immediately from that principle of human nature, which is so admirably unfolded in the *theory of moral sentiments, by Dr. A. Smith.* Jurymen are but arbiters under another name; and *arbitration* is the most natural, as well as the most excellent way of composing differences. The only difficulty perhaps was to transfer this method from civil to criminal causes. But after all, in establishing and regulating a mode of dispensing justice, which was dictated by feelings lodged in every bosom, there is nothing which we need imagine placed beyond the reach of minds little inured to reflection. Several nations, we know, inherited this invaluable blessing from their rude ancestors; and probably all enjoyed it in some form or other, till it was wrested from them by their oppressors.

" and of connecting words together in Syntax. Then " tenses and moods of verbs were to be contrived, " by which the circumstance of time, and the affec- " tions and dispositions of the human mind with re- " spect to the action of the verb, were to be ex- " pressed." (II. p. 489.) The language was besides to be made musical; and before every thing, it was necessary to have accomplished " that great work of " science, viz. analysis."

The universal *tendency to contraction*, is not less apparent in the Greek than in other languages: and the writers whom I have quoted in [illegible] instances, both prove and allow it, though in the formation of the language they seem only to think of the contrary process; a process without cause or motive, unless in very rare cases, and therefore contrary to nature. Lord M. gives us this gradation. From [illegible], (the original infinitive, according to him,)

come [illegible]

[illegible]

[illegible]

[illegible] (II. p. 507.)

So also, [illegible], [illegible], [illegible], [illegible]

Lennep. [illegible], [illegible], [illegible]

ἐξελάσειν, ἐξελάειν, ἐξελῶ.

for, [illegible], [illegible] — [illegible], [illegible]

Valckenaer

Valckenaer allows contraction in ſuch caſes as theſe, πιλεω—πλεω,—τιρεω,—τρεω—and hence we might eaſily have πλῶ and τρῶ.

Mr. Scheid ſupplies a great number of contractions both in Greek and Latin—as φανος, *fax, a torch* *. πανος, παξ: of *edo*, I eat, he obſerves, declinatio verbi per *es*, *eſt eſſe*, *eſtur*, hoc eſt, *edis*, *edit*, *edere*, *editur*, p. 342, where he explains why the *d* takes place of the *s*.—In a few inſtances, the perverted order of derivation, which I lay to the charge of theſe etymologiſts, is palpable. Thus, *a* κύω oſculor, *formatum eſt futurum* κύσω, et σ geminata, κύσσω. Now in this word, imitative of ſound, every one's ears will ſatisfy him, that κυσσω muſt have been before κυω, as being ſo much more expreſſive †.——Scaliger had derived "*mitto*" *I ſend*, from μῖτος, a *thread*, "quoniam qui mittit, elongat,"—No, ſays Mr. S., it comes from

* His ingenious obſervation on the very general word *facio*, deſerves to be quoted: *facio* proprie *in lucem profero, emitto, oſtendo*. . . . . *Unde jam ſtatim intelligi poterit, qui de causâ verbum facere adhibeatur tantum de* externis & loci *quaſi* expoſitis *actionibus; alterum vero*, agere *de* internis *proprie dicatur*, p. 328.

† Πτισσω, pinſo, *fortè pro* πισσω, a πιω, (ſee the Etymologicum,) is ſurely an example of the ſame perverted etymology, and many others might be enumerated.

μίω,

μίω, which is akin to μύω, and therefore signifies any motion, *quo* quid *elaretur* et *projiciatur*. The same sort of mistake perpetually occurs in the *Etymologicum*, where all the primitives have a *general* meaning assigned to them, and the derivatives a particular. Now it is obvious, that all significations must arise from particular perceptions, and the meaning of all words be analogically extended; we must first have a given motion, and then the term for *motus*, quo *quid*. Hence when it is said, that μυος, μυς, a *mouse*, comes from μυω *penetro*, this order must be the reverse of right, unless a word for *penetrate* had been derived from some other individual phænomenon.

But what overturns this whole system of analogical elongation at once, is a discovery of Mr. Scheid, to which Lennep contributed an hint, and the eastern languages a direct analogy: this discovery affords by far the most important elucidation of the structure of the Greek language, of any thing contained in the three volumes, of which he has been the publisher. Indeed, the observations of Mr. Scheid are, in general, much superior to those of his predecessors, especially to those of Valckenaer; and the superiority probably depends on his great knowledge of the oriental languages.

These

These languages, as he remarks, univerſally form the perſons of the præterite, by adding certain ſyllables of the ancient pronouns to their infinitive forms. Thus *Sjchabb* in Hebrew ſignifies *decumbere*, and *atta*, *tu*, and *attem*, *vos*; hence by coaleſcence and contraction, *sjchabb*-TA, *decubuiſti*, and *sjchabb*-TEM, *decubuiſtis*. In like manner he ſhews, that from the coaleſcence of εγω, εμες, εμι, αμες, (which as well as εμοι and εμε all ſtood for the firſt perſon ſingular,) with certain other words or ſounds, were formed the Greek verbs in -ω and -μι; as

Ἄω or ἄμι, for ἄεγω or ἄεμι *I breathe*, from the coaleſcence of the firſt vowel, (originally perhaps ſeveral times repeated, in imitation of the ſound of breathing or panting ἄ α α,) and εγω.—So alſo, from πτὺ, a ſound imitative of ſpitting and the ſame pronoun Πτύω or πτῦμι for πτυεγω, or πτυεμι. He goes through the other perſons of the verb, and ſhews, that they are compoſed of *adforming* pronouns and other ſounds. The Latin verbs in -m, (*inquam*, &c.) he obſerves, correſpond to the Greek in -μι. The infinitive is formed in the ſame way by the addition of -ειν to πτυ, &c. This is common ſenſe; here we have ſatisfactory reaſons aſſigned for each change; whereas Valckenaer and Lord Monboddo have both been led, by by their system of derivation, and each independently of the other, to assign a fortuitous and causeless origin to the verbs in μι, and also to mistake their relative antiquity. "There are at present in Greek," says Lord Monboddo, "two kinds of verbs, one terminating in -ω, the other in -μι: but it is evident, that these last verbs are derived from the circumflex verbs in -ῶ; and *that they were a variety in the form of the verbs, introduced in later times, and no part of the original constitution of the language.* "Accordingly in the most antient dialect of the Greek, I mean in the Latin, they are not to be found." (II. 515.) Nearly so Valckenaer— *a verbis in αω manarunt verba in ημι, a verbis in οω, verba in* ωμι (p. 16.). *In Homero*, says Lennep on the contrary, *longe plura hujus generis verba* (in μι) *quam in reliquis scriptoribus Græcis reperiuntur* (p. 113): he adds, that the Æolic dialect, having undergone less change than the Attic (that is, in fact, being older), has far more verbs in -μι.

The whole theory of the formation of persons and tenses, by changing letters and syllables, must be as false as it is unsatisfactory, and it assigns the reason of nothing. All the Greek persons and tenses and oblique cases must be explained by the anatomy of the

the words, as Mr. Scheid has explained them in ſome inſtances. I might juſt as well ſay, that A *ſcalp* is derived from TO *ſcalp*, by changing TO into A, as that ζευγνυμι is formed from ζευγνυω, by changing ω into μι, and ſo on in all tenſes, moods, and caſes. The argument from the analogy of the Greek words actually diſſected, corroborated as it is by the analogy of other languages, which like the Engliſh (as *I think, we think, you think, they think*) *prefix* inſtead of ſuffixing, in order to form the perſons of their verbs, is perfectly deciſive: nor is there any thing better than mere aſſertion to oppoſe to it. And Lennep eſtimates the aſſertions of grammarians at their full value, when he obſerves: *Id nimirum ſemper tenendum, in hoc ſtudiorum genere, parum aut nihil fere vidiſſe grammaticos, tam veteres quam recentiores; adeoque, nullo modo eorum placitis eſſe ſtandum, niſi tum quando ex ipſâ linguæ naturâ petita eſſe ea appareat* (p. 55.). Indeed, except as to the ſound of a language, it is indifferent whether theſe modifying words are prefixed or ſuffixed. In Swediſh, the articles are annexed to the end of the words; and this, I believe, is one reaſon, why that language is ſo much the moſt mellifluous (and of courſe the only one abounding in operas) of the whole northern ſiſter-hood. We may be aſ-

 ſured,

ſured, that ω was never metamorphoſed, as Valckenaer ſuppoſes (p. 44.), by any grammatical magic into εις, ει to make perſons, nor into ος or ρος to make nouns, as ωον, ωος, ωρος; the difference muſt depend upon the appoſition of different words, and the extermination perhaps of the laſt ſyllable of the firſt, and the firſt ſyllable of the laſt, of the coaleſcing words.

Hence it appears that Lord Monboddo, as well as the Hemſterhuſian ſchool, were groſsly deceived in ſuppoſing the *verb* or verbs, to be the parent word of the whole Greek language; the verbs or words which we conjugate, were of late formation; and aroſe as the language was ground down by uſe. Nouns, or the names of perceptions, are, in truth, the only ▬ part of ſpeech: from them all was derived. Several years ago, a gentleman in Oxford, whoſe minute ſkill in languages and general juſtneſs of views, are not ſufficiently known beyond the circle of his friends, ſhewed me by inſtances, like that adduced by Mr. Scheid, *that the Hebrew language has no verbs*. In the ſame ſenſe, the Saxon languages are without verbs; and the Greek verbs are compoſed of nouns. Accordingly, Mr. Tooke very juſtly obſerves, that "a conſideration of *ideas*, or of the *mind*, or of "*things*, relative to the parts of ſpeech, will lead us

"no

"no farther than to *nouns*; i. e. the signs of those "impressions or names of ideas. The other part of "speech, the *verb*, must be accounted for from the "necessary use of it in communication. It is in "fact, the communication itself; and therefore well "denominated Ῥῆμα, *dictum*. For the verb is *quod* "*loquimur*, the noun, *de quo*." (p. 71.): to make a verb, or to communicate, we put together the name of a thing and of an action or passion. The mode of expression of children and Africans frequently exemplifies this remark.

To conclude a contest with chimæras, which affords no immediate satisfaction, and in its most favourable issue, can confer little honour; I shall quote from Mr. Scheid a passage, in which he finally rejects the whole *analogy* of his masters; and if we had none but preternatural means offered to our choice, I should, with him, prefer revelation to the supposition of rude men falling upon this milliner's method of fashioning a language, by sticking letters in the middle or at the end of little primitives, in order to puff them out. *Equidem fateor, subtilem nimis mihi sæpe visam fuisse istam quam diximus, derivandi rationem*; *quasi vero antiquissimi Græci normam hanc* de communi consilio, in sermonis sui amplificatione, sibi legissent;

ut ab ἄω insertâ aliquâ vocali de quinque *vocalibus, efformarent ἀάω, ἀέω, ἀίω, ἀόω, ἀύω, ab ἕω, ἑάω, ἑέω, ἑίω, ἑόω, ἑύω. Rudibus mortalibus, (si vel maxime linguas humanum opus esse existimes,* quod nunquam ego crediderim) *antequam lingua jam constituta esset, eam tribuere ἀκρίβειαν, quæ vix a philosophis, novam forte linguam condituris, expectari possit, id vero nimium mihi videtur esse, in hoc antiquitatis studio; neque id valuisse Lennepium, summosque ipsius præceptores, Hemsterhusium et Valckenarium,* facile inducor ut credam (p. 491.) Mr. S. supposes ἄαι the old dative of ἄα, which is formed from ἄω, to have given rise to ἀάω, and so forth.

The physical consideration of the vowels will go a great way towards explaining the facts upon which this system of analogy is founded. In the different languages of Europe, A, E, I, O, U, represent some scores, and perhaps some hundreds of sounds, varying by imperceptible gradations; and it is evident from anatomy, that such sounds may be varied without end. From the affinity of the vowels, and of several of the consonants *, it happens that the same sound is in

* Lennep's Idea, if he be the author of it, of arranging the letters of the alphabet, according to their affinity, is ingenious. He places, for instance, G next to K, B to P, D to T, and so on.

writing

writing reprefented very differently. Before the invention of the art of printing, it was perhaps impoffible to introduce an uniform orthography; though the more a language was written, the more it would approach towards uniformity in this refpect. In moft of thofe cafes therefore, where the vowels are fuppofed to have been feverally inferted, we have, in fact, only one word differently fpelled: and this difference of fpelling will be more firmly eftablifhed, the longer the ftates, that fpeak a common language, continue independant of one another. Had all Germany groaned for ages under the tyranny of one defpot, we fhould not have had the difference of orthography, which ftill prevails between the Saxon, Swifs, Pruffian and Auftrian writers. Moreover, in every thing we do, we proceed by analogy, and imitation is the mould in which we are all caft. Now it is a circumftance of great fingularity and importance, that in the improvement of the Greek language, and in the gradual contraction of Greek words, this invariable tendency of human nature was not difturbed by the influence of any more polifhed language. Thefe feveral caufes will, I think, fully account for thofe groups of refembling founds which are obferved in that language. And fimilarity of conftruction, being founded upon a principle, common to all mankind, muſt prevail to a certain extent in other languages as well as in the Greek; and as Lennep juſtly obſerves; analogia, *ex ipſa hominis natura manans, in omnibus omnino linguis, pro diverſâ indole earum, diverſa quidem, in ſingulis tamen, æquali modo, per omnes earundem partes, regnat conſtantiſſimè.* It may appear extraordinary, that a perſon, who makes ſo many juſt ſingle obſervations, ſhould adopt a ſyſtem ſo improbable and ſo deſtitute of proof. But the phænomenon is not unprecedented. The facts, adduced by other theoriſts, have ſometimes been ſubverſive of their ſyſtem.

NOTE II.

On the Spirit and Tendency of the Doctrines of the Επεα Πτεροεντα, *and on the Merit of the Author as a Discoverer.*

CONsidering the long delusions which words have supported, the deadly animosities, public and private, to which they have given rise, and how much genius they have rendered useless or pernicious to mankind, *grammar* may be numbered among the most important of all pursuits. That work, therefore, in which Mr. Tooke has revealed so much of the structure of language, appeared to me, on its first publication, one of the most valuable, as well as one of the most ingenious productions, that ever issued from the press; except Mr. Locke's Essay, I consider it as that which has most contributed towards the theory of our intellectual faculties. Whatever may be thought of their *value*, no one, I believe, capable of underſtanding the proofs, will heſitate to admit the *truth* of the doctrines it contains.

But moſt fortreſſes have ſome weak or unguarded ſpot. When a theory is eſtabliſhed by incontrovertible evidence, the uſual mode of hoſtility is to diſpute the author's claim to diſcovery. Should he be in any way obnoxious, this kind of attack is not likely, on that account, to be carried on with leſs than ordinary vigour.

It has accordingly been ſaid, that although his philoſophy of language be true, yet little or no credit is due to Mr. Tooke, ſince it had previouſly been taught by others. If ſo, Mr. T. was either acquainted with their works, or he was not. According to the latter ſuppoſition, we may conſole him by ſome ſlight commendations of his ingenuity, but, in a ſhort time, we ſhall think no more about him. Our tribute of admiration and of gratitude, will all be paid, as juſtly due, to his predeceſſors. But if he was acquainted with their diſcoveries, then notwithſtanding any trifling corrections or additions he may have made, his attempt to deceive us, and defraud our inſtructors and benefactors of their reward, will ſuppreſs every ſentiment but indignation.

The

The indictment againſt Mr. T., may be laid in the name of Skinner and his brethren, of Lord Monboddo, or the Dutch ſchool of etymologiſts.

The ſhare in the Ἔπεα Πτερόεντα due to Sanctius, Voſſius, Skinner, or Junius, who are always, I believe, fairly quoted, will vaniſh altogether upon a juſt eſtimation: nor will any equitable critic, acquainted with the progreſs of diſcovery, dwell a moment upon this charge. It has always happened, that certain facts belonging to an extenſive theory have been noticed, and certain hints, which when they have *afterwards* been adverted to, might be ſuppoſed to ſuggeſt it, have been thrown out, long before the theory itſelf was fully formed. This can hardly fail to be the caſe with all juſt theories. A man need not poſſeſs a very obſervant eye, nor a very generalizing mind, to notice a ſew out of a multitude of facts, which he has every day before him, and to ſuſpect ſome connection between them. The predeceſſors of Harvey were ſo perfectly acquainted with the proofs from which Harvey deduced the circulation of the blood, that Haller wonders how they could have failed, eſpecially one of them, to draw the concluſion. But Haller does not the leſs, on this account, acknowledge the genius of Harvey.

Harvey. If it be true that Skinner's IF spoke so plainly and so loud in behalf of himself and his kindred, why was the cry lost upon Johnson, Lowth, Harris, Monboddo, as well as our other grammarians and lexicographers of high and low degree. It was because Skinner's derivation, if it shines at all, shines with a reflected light—it was because it is not every man, who has eyes, that can perceive.

Lord Monboddo will not infringe even so much as Skinner upon the grammatical reputation of Mr. Tooke. Skinner's merit does amount to something, though the sum be scarce large enough to be appreciated. Lord Monboddo's is a solitary cypher. The following passage occurs in his second volume, published in 1774, and is that upon which his claim must be founded. "I prefer that division of the "parts of speech, that has been given both by Plato "and Aristotle, into *noun* and *verb*; and I will en-"deavour to shew, that all the other parts of speech "above-mentioned, (viz. the eight commonly enu-"merated) may be fitly referred to one or other of "these two." In a note his lordship informs us, that "Aristotle has given this division in his book "of interpretation, and Plato in the Sophist. It is "true,

" true, that Ariſtotle . . . . . in his popular work " upon poetry, ch. 20. has given us another diviſion, " more ſuited to the capacity of thoſe for whom he " wrote that book, viz. into *noun*, *verb*, *article* and " *conjunction*." (II. 28.) To write falſhood and nonſenſe for the edification of the people, has indeed been a practice common enough ſince the days of Ariſtotle, and probably before him. I do not, however, in the preſent caſe, give Ariſtotle the credit of any ſuch laudable intention. I rather ſuppoſe that he was not acquainted with any one of thoſe phænomena which betray the nature of language; if ſo, his fluctuation between different ſurmiſes will appear natural enough. His expreſſions would undoubtedly have been preciſe and uniform, had he entertained but a ſuſpicion of the nature of *particles*. Lord Monboddo certainly repeats the opinion without comprehending the ſubject any better than Ariſtotle, and no where in his very prolix *Analyſis of the formal part of language*, which, after all, is no analyſis, nor any thing in any degree approaching towards an analyſis, does he offer either proof or preſumption in favour of his hypotheſis. He even adjures the reader by his candour, not to impute to him any ſuch deſign. " The

" candid

" candid reader, ſays he, will not underſtand that I " mean to ſay, that conjunctions, prepoſitions, and " ſuch like words, which are rather the pegs and " nails that faſten the ſeveral parts of the language, " than the language itſelf, are derived from verbs, or " are derivatives of any kind, but he will underſtand " that I mean the names of things, which are pro- " perly the words of a language." (II. p. 188.) This is then what his lordſhip's doctrine amounts to, compared with that of former grammarians. They, many of them, reckoned eight parts of ſpeech; the *noun* and *verb* among others. Lord M. reckons two only, all the while merely repeating Plato and Ariſtotle; —and theſe are the *noun* and *verb*. As to the particles, wherein lay all the difficulty, he ſays, they are *pegs* and *nails*, *not the language itſelf*, *not properly the words of a language*. And when he conjectures, that the verb is the parent word of the whole Greek language, he muſt mean of the whole eight parts of ſpeech, ſix excepted. Whatever may be Mr. T.'s dexterity, as a literary thief, he never ſtole an atom of his doctrine from Lord Monboddo. Nor do I imagine his lordſhip would venture an oath, or even an affirmation, that any article in the Επεα Πτεροεντα is his pro-

property, except what is duly marked with his lordship's name *. When he comes to explain the pronoun, this is his philosophy. "If either the speaker "or the hearer be the subject of the discourse, there "is no more ado than to invent two words to design "and distinguish them from one another. And "these words are called *pronouns*: viz. of the first "and second person." In explaining the origin of the pronoun of the third person, he is equally luminous. Having premised, that if there be an object in question, of which the hearer knows nothing beforehand, we can convey no knowledge of this object to him but by shewing it; "but suppose the object, he "continues, had been mentioned before in the dis-"course, and that in this way he has come to the "knowledge of it, any word marking a reference "to the object before-mentioned, and denoting that "it is the same with the object now mentioned, will "be sufficient to single out and distinguish that ob-

* The only possible exception is in the latter part of this sentence. "The art of language appears to consist in four things: "1. In expressing accurately and distinctly all the conceptions "of the human mind. 2. *In doing this by as few words as pos-"sible.*" (II. p. 6.)

"ject

" ject from others. And here we have another pro-" noun of the third person, which serves to distinguish " subjects of the conversation that are not present." (II. p. 49.) According to Lord M.'s doctrine, when a man was in want of a pronoun, there was no more ado than to invent one; but *how* he set about this invention! why truly, sagacious reader, this trivial and accessory problem he leaves to thee to solve. It seems clear, from his own terms, that the pronoun is not any more than the conjunctions, &c. one among the parts of speech which he would derive from the verb; and nothing, for I will not cavil about trifling inaccuracies, would have been wanting to the theory, if, as he has entitled the particles, the *pegs* and *nails*, it had pleased him to christen the pronouns, the *finger-posts* of language.

Mr. Harris accounts for the observation of Plato and Aristotle in this manner. " Plato in his Sophist " mentions only two (parts of speech), the *noun* and " the *verb*. Aristotle mentions no more, where he " treats of propositions. Not that those acute philo-" sophers were ignorant of the other parts, but they " spoke with reference to *logic* or *dialectic*, consider-" ing the essence of speech as contained in these two, " because *these alone* combined make a perfect *affir-*

" *tive* sentence, which none of the rest without them " are able to effect. Hence therefore Aristotle in his " *treatise of poetry*, (where he was to lay down the " elements of a more variegated speech) adds the *ar-* " *ticle* and *conjunction*, &c." In a note Mr. Harris quotes Priscian and Boetius (Hermes, p. 33.); the former observes, *hæ solæ (part. orat. nempe,* NOMEN *et* VERBUM) *etiam per se conjunctæ plenam faciunt orationem*; and the latter declares it to be Aristotle's meaning, that a simple enunciative sentence may be expressed by *noun* and *verb* alone. I know not whether this supposition will rescue Aristotle from the imputation of a discovery, but we may be certain, I think, that he did not speak with any knowledge of the structure of language. And if there be any thing in him or in Plato, (for we must quit Lord Monboddo, and —*integros accedere fontes*) capable of throwing light upon the subject, why was it left for ages unapplied? Their works have been long enough before the world, and been more than sufficiently studied. Considered merely as a commentator of Aristotle and Plato, Mr. T.'s merit will, I conceive, be just as great, as if we suppose, that his opinions were suggested by his own observation of language.

It

It is impossible to think of the Dutch etymologists without a lively sense of gratitude. Yet if we consider Mr. T.'s freedom from the hypotheses with which they are encumbered, that important application which he makes of his doctrine to the illustration of Mr. Locke's Essay, and the light he every where throws on collateral subjects, they will appear to be at least half a century behind our countryman in the philosophy of language. Nevertheless, they have collected many useful materials; and some architect, more skilful than themselves, would have arranged them into a just system at some future period.

Before I proceed to shew how little probable it is that he should have had any knowledge of their researches, let me remind the reader, that within the last twenty or thirty years, persons, in different countries, have oftener than once fallen upon the same, and that a very important and unexpected, discovery. Nor in these cases has there been any suspicion of foul play on either side.

The discovery of oxygene air, which was made about the same time, both by Dr. Priestley and Mr. Scheele, affords one remarkable example of this kind. And these coincidences will occur more frequently, as the human mind is roufed to activity in a greater number of different countries.

Now Mr. Tooke's *letter to* Mr. Dunning, was publifhed in 1778. That letter, I am told, has been long out of print, and I have never feen it. But the author informs us, that it contains the fubftance of the 6th, 7th, 8th, and 9th chapters of his later work. Thefe chapters treat of the word *that*, of *conjunctions*, of the *etymology of the Englifh conjunctions*, and of *prepofitions*. And they offer befides, a great variety of the moft acute and ingenious obfervations, together with examples of *refolution*, fuch as it would be in vain to feek in any other writer upon language.

No perfon will hefitate a moment to believe, that the author had formed his fyftem of language at a period, when he had explained all that was difficult in the particles. What *time* he will allow for the formation of this body of grammatical knowledge, every reader muft judge from his own experience in difcoveries, or the beft obfervations he may have been able to make upon the fpeed of others in difcovery. One thing I hold as certain, that when a man of genius has fatisfied himfelf of any new truth, he is, in general, very loath to begin to mould it into a fhape fit for public infpection, and advances very flowly with this task. This aversion to the drudgery of drawing out a theory in form, whether it be pride, or habit, or indolence, seems sometimes for a long time, and sometimes finally, to have withheld valuable discoveries from the world.

Now this date of the letter to Mr. Dunning, to neglect every consideration, cuts off the pretensions of Mr. Villoison's publication of an extract from a MS. work of Lennep; for Mr. Villoison did not, I think, publish Longus's Pastorals, till 1778 *; and before

* Mr. Villoison had desired Mr. Scheid to procure him a MS. copy of part of Lennep's Lectures. "Ejus rei exitus tunc fuit, ut approbatâ a te quam maxime," says the latter, addressing himself to the former, Hemsterhusianæ scholæ disciplinâ, dignissimum haberes Lennepii opusculum, cujus partem haud ignobilem—— tuæ Longi Pastoralium editioni insereres, *ut non Belgarum tantummodo nostrorum privatis usibus Lennepiana hæc inservirent, sed ad cæterarum quoque gentium Gallorum præsertim, Hispanorum et Italorum* (ipsa tua verba sunt) *pervenirent notitiam.* (*Dedication of Valckenaer's Observations*, &c.) Mr. Burgess afterwards reprinted the same extract in Dawes's *Miscell. Critica*. In the prolegom. to the Etymologicum, p. 1. Mr. Scheid expresses his consciousness, how little all these researches were known out of Holland. A surreptitious edition of Lennep *de Analogia* was printed, I know not where nor when, never having seen it. But it obtained no sort of attention in foreign countries, and was not valued even in Holland.

before this date, the Dutch Analogy had made, as they own themselves, little or no noise abroad.

In the numerous quartos of Schultens, some excellent observations on *particles*, seem, indeed, to have lain hid. I would not swear, for I cannot know, that Mr. Tooke never, in his researches, stumbled upon these passages. But against this supposition a presumption arises from the size and number of the volumes of Schultens, as well as from the little attention the observations in question obtained abroad; no particular marks of imitation are pointed out; we have only a bare possibility. And against this we have strong internal evidence in the peculiar features of Mr. T.'s work. The air and manner of the *Diversions of Purley*, strike me at least as altogether original. The property of the most valuable parts of the work, which seem entirely to be overlooked in the charge, is not disputed; and the whole work is so much of a piece, that the author of the best part was undoubtedly ca-

Holland. *Neque multo melior conditio fuit libri Lennepiani; qui et ipse, saepissime, ab imperitis, negligentibusve aut stupidis hominibus ita descriptus est, ut vix jam cum jucunditate aliquâ legi posset nauseamque crearet eorum usuris. Testis esto editio optimi hujus libelli prima, quae sub falso Londini nomine . . . . . foedissimis mendis commaculata fuit, atque adeo merito contemtui est habita.*

 pable

pable of being the author of the rest; and not only so, but if, as he says, and as is abundantly probable, his philosophy of ideas, independently of etymology, afforded him a glimpse of his philosophy of language; and if he had long considered the greater part of Mr. Locke's Essay, as a treatise upon words, he *must necessarily have discovered the nature of particles*, though not a single one had ever been investigated before. Passages innumerable in his work, to which there is nothing similar in the works of these other writers, prove that he was equal to the whole discovery, and that he was in the train to make it. Nothing indeed can appear more evident, than the etymology of the greater number of particles, now we have been taught how to trace them to their source; nor need any one be surprized that he, who failed after a chart so much more correct, should have made so much greater progress.

From the former part of this, and from the foregoing note, it may be collected how different Mr. Tooke's general views of language are from the views of all those writers whom I have quoted besides. In order fully to enable the reader to judge, between the spirit of his philosophy and that of Lord Monboddo, I have extracted from each a passage, treating of the

same

ſame part of ſpeech. This experiment of juxtapoſition, I can aſſure him, is fairly made; and it will ſhew whether the one has gone beyond the commonplace futility of grammar, and how widely the other has extended his views beyond mere etymology, and what an admirable rationale he gives of the *manner of ſignification* of words.

Lord Monboddo.

"Prepoſitions I likewiſe claſs under verbs, as they denote relations of things; not abſtractedly, for then they would be nouns, but inherent in their ſubjects, ſo that they are qualities which are not conſidered as having a ſeparate exiſtence. The chief uſe of them, as it appears to me, is to expreſs relations, which could not be conveniently expreſſed by the caſes of nouns, ſuch as place, ſituation, order, and many other connections of things, which are obſerved by grammarians, in the ſignifications they give to the ſeveral prepoſitions. *They are of very great uſe in ſyntax, and govern a caſe, whereby we know the word to which they refer.*

To know the preciſe meaning of the prepoſitions in the Greek language, and to be able to diſtinguiſh the proper from the figurative ſignification of them, is is a matter of great nicety . . . . the uſe of them in compoſition gives a peculiar beauty and accuracy of expreſſion to the Greek language. There are commonly enough two of them, and ſometimes three, in compoſition with their verbs, by which they deſcribe ſo minutely the action of the verb, that it is really a kind of painting. Thus Homer, in deſcribing water coming out of the foot of a rock, uſes the word *ὑπ-εκ-προ-ρεειν*, by which is deſcribed, firſt its coming from *below*, then its coming *out*, or *guſhing*, and laſtly, its running forward.

The adverb, as the name imports, is a ſort of adjunct of the verb, and appears to me to be ſuch a ſupplement of the verb, as the prepoſition is to the noun.

As ſingle words are connected together by the means of caſes and prepoſitions, it is fit alſo that ſentences, and members of ſentences, ſhould be connected together; and for that purpoſe, a ſet of words have been invented, called *conjunctions*, which though they may ſeem often only to connect words, yet it is truly ſentences that they connect. . . . . . I ſhall only obſerve, that though they all go by the name of *conjunctions*, ſome of them *connect* by disjoining, not by joining." II. 175-8.—For this laſt obſervation, and many such besides, I suppose every school-boy, who should not happen to have them in his grammar will be ready to acknowledge his obligations.

MR. TOOKE.

" As the necessity of the *article*, or of some equivalent invention follows from the impossibility of having in language a distinct name, or particular *term*, for each particular individual *idea*; so does the necessity of the *preposition*, or of some equivalent invention, follow from the impossibility of having in language, a distant *complex term* for each different *collection of ideas*, which we may have occasion to put together in discourse. The addition or subtraction of *any one* idea to or from a collection, makes it a different collection: and, if there were degrees of impossibility, it is still more impossible to use in language a different and distinct *complex term* for each different and distinct *collection of ideas*, than it is to use a distinct *particular term*, for each particular and individual idea. To supply the place therefore of the complex terms which are wanting in a language, is the preposition employed, by whose aid *complex* terms are prevented from being infinite or too numerous, and are used only

only for those collections of ideas which we have most frequently occasion to mention in discourse. And this end is obtained in the most simple manner in the world. For having occasion in communication, to mention a collection of ideas, for which there is no one simple *complex* term in the language, we either take that complex term which includes the greatest number, though not *all*, of the ideas we would communicate, or else we take that complex term, which includes *all*, and the fewest ideas *more* than those we would communicate; and then by the help of the preposition, we make up the deficiency in the one case, or retrench the superfluity in the other.—For instance,

1. *A house* WITH *a party-wall.*

2. *A house* WITHOUT *a party-wall.*

In the first instance, the complex term is deficient: the preposition directs to add what is wanting. In the second instance, the complex term is redundant: the preposition directs to take away what is superfluous.

If to one of our modern grammarians, I should say—A *house* JOIN—he would ask me—JOIN what? but he would not contend that JOIN is an indeclinable word, and has no meaning of its own; because he knows

knows that it is the imperative of the verb, the other parts of which are ſtill in uſe; and its own meaning is clear to him, though the ſentence is not compleated. If inſtead of JOIN, I ſhould ſay to him—A *houſe* WITH, he would ſtill aſk the ſame queſtion—WITH *what?*" Mr. T. then ſhews from etymology, that his inſtances ſtand thus:

" 1. *A houſe* JOIN *a party-wall.*

2. *A houſe* BE-OUT *a party-wall.*"

Now this full and clear diſplay of the manner of ſignification of words, by which the plan, begun by Mr. Locke, has been nearly compleated, conſtitutes, in my apprehenſion, the great and diſtinguiſhing merit of the *Επεα Πτεροεντα*, above all other works on language. I find none of theſe comprehenſive views in the Dutch etymologiſts; and though they have contributed much to unfold the manner of ſignification of the hitherto ſo imperfectly underſtood particles in the Greek and Latin, the Oriental and Dutch languages, they have but ſupplied materials to the *philoſopher*; their labours may be conſidered as bearing to the theory of *language*, the ſame relation which the noting down of individual appearances in the heavens bears to the theory of aſtronomy. The only

N just

just principle they were able to deduce I have quoted above (p. 6, *note*), and this principle they were so little able to apply, that as we have seen, they have reversed the progress of language, both in the formation of words and the genealogy of significations. As to Lord Monboddo, his doctrine of the operations of mind is directly contrary to that of Mr. Locke, as it has been corrected by the author of Επεα Πτεροεντα; who justly observes, "that his Lordship and his fautors will do well to contend stoutly and obstinately "for their doctrine of language, for they are menaced "with a greater danger than *they* will at first apprehend; for if they give up their doctrine of language, they will not be able to make even a battle "for their metaphysics: the very term *metaphysic* "being nonsense; and all the systems of it, and controversies concerning it, that are or have been in "the world, being founded on the grossest ignorance "of words, and of the nature of speech." If therefore Mr. Tooke had not discovered a single etymology, which till it is proved, every impartial person will beg to be excused from believing; if his admirable resolution of THAT, and the proof he has given of the steadiness of signification of words in the case

of

of FOR (a word, which had so much perplexed the lexicographers *,) were struck out of his book, it would still retain an immense value. It would have the merit, 1. of purifying learning from the last blemishes and obscurities left upon it by the study of *universals*. 2. By exposing the futile falshoods of grammar, it will contribute to the amendment of education, a work of mercy which will redeem a multitude of sins; and, 3. It will eventually deliver mankind from those fierce and fatal contentions, for which ignorance of the foundation of knowledge, and of the structure of language, supplied the pretext. The more information, indeed, we acquire on this and other subjects, and the more pains we take to form opinions by the help of our own unbiassed reflections, the more shall we possess of that equity of mind, on which depends the charity of thought and action. Solid knowledge

* Greek scholars will now be saved the trouble of studying the fatiguing *minutiæ* of Vigerus, Hoogeveen, &c. This mode of resolution, (the *corporeal* signification of *particles* being given, and Mr. Scheid will supply that), will do away the supposed variation of sense in the same word, and the caprice of idiom; than which no study, I imagine, can be more perplexing, more burdensome to the memory, or more barren of useful instruction.

humanizes

humanizes, without enfeebling or rendering effeminate, the character.

I may be allowed to add, that I have no other reason for respecting Mr. Tooke, than as he is the teacher of truth. The temptations to decry him are obvious enough: I know of none to praise him beyond what he deserves; and if it shall be proved that he has been guilty of the greatest crime, which, as the writer of a work on language, he could commit, I shall not only conceive proper detestation of his conduct, but shall be grateful to any person who shall inform me, to whom my respect is due; for this sentiment I shall assuredly ever retain for the discoverer of truths so important.——As to Mr. Tooke, if after reading these remarks, he should require an apology for the freedom which a stranger has taken with his name, I confess myself unable to make him one that will be satisfactory, unless it be already made.

THE END.

ERRATA.

P. 19, l. 17, for *a such*, r. *such a*. P. 23, l. 9, for *that*, r. *as to*. P. 26, l. 7, for *angels*, r. *angles*. P. 33, last line, for *extremity*, r. *extremities*. P. 47, l. [illegible]6, for *on*, r. *as*. P. 49, after *bars*, insert *are*. P. 51, l. 15, for *pencil*, r. *pencils*. P. 54, l. 2, dele *to*. P. 108, after *former*, insert *uncertainty*. P. 140, l. 13, for *quoted in a thousand instances*, r, *quoted, in . . . instances*. P. 146, l. 15, dele *true*.

www.ingramcontent.com/pod-product-compliance
Lightning Source LLC
Chambersburg PA
CBHW020536270326
41927CB00006B/603

* 9 7 8 3 7 4 2 8 2 4 4 8 6 *